Why *Tyrannosaurus* But Not *If*?

The Dyslexic Blueprint for the Future of Education

RICHARD WHITEHEAD

Why *Tyrannosaurus* But Not *If?*
American English edition

Copyright © 2017 by Richard Whitehead

All rights reserved. No portion of this book may be copied, retransmitted, reposted, duplicated, or otherwise used without the express written approval of the author, except by reviewers who may quote brief excerpts in connection with a review.

Davis Dyslexia Association International, the DDAI logo, the phrases Davis Dyslexia Correction, Davis Symbol Mastery, Davis Orientation Counseling, Davis Math Mastery, Davis Learning Strategies, and Dyslexia The Gift are trademarks and service marks of Ronald D. Davis and DDAI. They may only be used in commerce by individuals trained and currently licensed by Davis Dyslexia Association International.

ISBN: 1912355019

ISBN-13: 978-1912355013

Cover design and "three parts of a word" graphics by Michaël Amos
http://michaelamos.uk/

Printed and bound in the United States of America.
First edition, July 2017.

Published by Create-A-Word Books Ltd
47 – 49 Church Street, Malvern, Worcestershire WR14 2AA, United Kingdom

Visit www.whytyrannosaurusbutnotif.com

DEDICATION

To Ronald Dell Davis.

An extraordinary educator
on whose wisdom most of this book is based.

Table of Contents

FOREWORD i

PREFACE v

PART I – WHY *TYRANNOSAURUS* BUT NOT *IF*?

Chapter 1: 'I Don't Understand It – He Can Read *Tyrannosaurus* But He Gets Stuck On *If*!'   1

Chapter 2: Working Backward from the Later Years: Observations of a Secondary School Teacher   20

Chapter 3: Words and Pictures: Verbal and Trans-Verbal Thinking   36

Chapter 4: To Sound or Not To Sound? That Is The Primary Question   50

Chapter 5: What Reading Is   64

Chapter 6: ADHD and the Processing Speed Conundrum   80

Chapter 7: Working Memory, or Feeling Memory?   96

PART II - THE TYRANNOSAURUS UNLEASHED

Chapter 8: The Davis Learning Strategies   116

Chapter 9: Priming the Mind - Davis Focusing Strategies   124

Chapter 10: Picturing Words - Davis Symbol Mastery   128

Chapter 11: The End of the Reading Wars   144

Chapter 12: Regular as Clockwork - A Creative Approach to Learning to Tell the Time   152

Chapter 13: Place Value   180

Chapter 14: Chemistry - Introducing Moles   192

Chapter 15: Pulling it All Together   198

BIBLIOGRAPHY   202

INDEX   213

GOING FURTHER   217

Table of Figures

Fig. 1: The three parts of a word 8

Fig. 2: Shaywitz' research into dyslexic and non-dyslexic brain activity during reading. Source: Dr Maria Luisa Lorusso 12

Fig. 3: A phonic responder's route in reading 14

Fig. 4: The typical dyslexic route in reading 15

Fig. 5: The block that typically confronts a dyslexic reader when a word's meaning does not evoke a mental image 16

Fig. 6: Example of an electronic mind map for subject revision 30

Fig. 7: The problem with phonics for learners with low phonological awareness 58

Fig. 8: The problem with phonics for learners with visual dyslexia 60

Fig. 9: The problem with phonics for learners with attention focus issues 61

Fig. 10: A reconstruction of the Stroop Test 73

Fig. 11: Davis Learning Strategies and basic sight words. 75

Fig. 12: Davis Learning Strategies and basic sight words. 76

Fig. 13: Davis Learning Strategies and GATE referrals 77

Fig. 14: The top row of the Symbol Digit Modalities Test (Smith, 1982) 82

Fig. 15: The Davis-Tzivanakis technique for mastery of the concept of 'left' 105

Fig. 16: The Davis Alphabet Mastery technique 106

Fig. 17: Symbol Mastery of puppy: 'a young dog' 137

ACKNOWLEDGMENTS

My heartfelt thanks go to all the dear friends and colleagues without whose help, advice and support this book would not have come about. Especial thanks to Abigail, Alice, Amanda, Caroline, Janice, Lynne, Mike, Ron – and above all, to my dear wife Margarita.

A big thankyou also to Michaël Amos for his patience and inspiration while creating the cover and interior designs.

Foreword
by Ronald D. Davis

In my book, *The Gift of Dyslexia*, I wrote of a little boy who asked God not to make him sit in the corner any more. In one sense, that little boy represented my own experience as a child who could neither read nor write and was labelled 'uneducatably mentally retarded'. In another way, he represented all the boys and girls who, over the centuries, have found they were unable to learn from books at school and have experienced shame, humiliation, and sometimes physical punishment as a result.

It would be nice to think that, nearly a quarter of a century later, the little boy's prayer has been answered. In some ways, perhaps it has. Back then, the idea that dyslexia might stem from a gift seemed outlandish to most. Since then, the notion of special dyslexic talents has spread far and wide. Dyslexics who excel in their profession are celebrated in books, on the Internet, and in Youtube videos, bringing hope and inspiration to millions of others.

And yet, there are still millions of little boys and girls across the world who struggle to learn. Sometimes, their parents or teachers try to boost their confidence by pointing out how many dyslexics have succeeded in life. However, most of our educational models lack the know-how to show these children how to harness their natural talent in order to master whatever they wish to learn. As a result, even today, many of these children turn into adults who go through life believing they are stupid when, in fact, this couldn't be further from the truth.

For centuries, the dream of helping lost, demoralized girls and boys to unlock their talents and discover a love of learning has drawn young men and women into teaching. In an age when many spend their working lives behind a computer screen, teachers are in direct daily contact with children and young people, charged with the task of fulfilling that very dream. Sometimes, a teacher of exceptional insight and talent finds that this dream comes true. Yet far too often, and through no fault of their own, teachers repeatedly fail to engage their struggling learners and become demoralized and jaded. The model by which they were taught to teach has let them down.

Parents of struggling learners are in a similar position. They, too, are driven by a passionate desire to help, nurture and protect their offspring. When they have a child who struggles to learn, they do the best that they can to help. For the most part, though, they too are limited by the educational models by which they themselves were taught at school. When these models fail to work for their children, they go through a potent mixture of frustration, confusion and inadequacy. With tragic irony, and despite the best of intentions, some of the resulting stress may well be transferred onto the child.

That is why this book is so important. Struggling dyslexic children need teachers and parents who are not just well-meaning, but also skilled in guiding them towards learning methods that work for *them*. The skills required are simple, but they challenge some existing educational paradigms. Therefore, they need to be coupled with compelling fresh insight into how dyslexics think and, consequently, how they learn. This book provides both – and in doing so, it offers a key that could unlock learning for the little boy in the corner and for millions of other innovative young thinkers.

Preface

I first entered a classroom as a teacher in my mid-twenties. It was a sobering experience. Passionate as I had always been to learn – as a school pupil, and then as a university student – it surprised me that there were so many children in my classes whom I simply couldn't reach. With the vigorous naivety of youth, I stayed up late and rose early, preparing detailed, sequential lessons that I thought would fascinate my classes. In delivering the lessons, I was fixated on the knowledge I was trying to impart and sometimes missed the reactions of the children I was trying to teach. Some of my lessons were great. Others were mediocre at best. My apologies to everyone who sat through some of the latter ones. I was trying hard and did not know how to do better.

In those perplexing early days, I noticed that certain learners were especially resistant to my teaching. One girl was particularly adept at slipping out of the classroom without handing in her homework. When she did hand in work, it was minimalistic – about a quarter of the expected length, with prolific errors made in even the shortest, most common words. As their teen years approached, some of these learners would be transformed from quiet, underachieving children into loud, over-assertive individuals whose behavior expressed that they were prisoners in my classroom, staying in the room because the law of the land required them to, but convinced now of their inability to learn anything of value there and largely unaware of the effect of their conduct on the learning of others. Yet others tried desperately hard, but their academic progress was painstakingly slow and fitful. Some would spend hours on end producing neat, well-written homework, but their grades would plummet in formal tests and exams. Over time, repeated exam and test failure would damage their self-esteem, sometimes producing 'exam phobia', an anxiety response before and during tests that would make their results still worse.

Later, after a brief period in the financial sector, I had the privilege of training in the Davis Dyslexia methods and then working one-to-one with children and adults who struggled with reading, writing, mathematics and/or paying due attention to the world around them. The Davis methods were conceived by Ronald Davis, a dyslexic individual who learnt to read and write in his late thirties and then went on to develop a new paradigm for tailored, dyslexia-friendly education. Davis outlined his approach in his book The Gift of Dyslexia, which quickly became an international best-seller. Through this work, my understanding of how dyslexics think, and therefore learn, grew exponentially.

Eight years later, I returned to classroom teaching and, ultimately, to the role of Special Education Coordinator in a British independent secondary school. I encountered many fellow-teachers – in my own school, and on training courses – who were hungry for fresh, meaningful and effective guidance on how to teach struggling learners. Many had received a derisory amount of guidance on special education from their teacher training – my own training course provided just one lecture on the topic, delivered in 'death-by-PowerPoint' style by a well-intentioned but uninspiring lecturer who was interrupted, one hour into her two-hour delivery, by pleas from the audience for a restroom break. Even tailored special education teacher training can be turgid and theoretical, with little emphasis placed on practical delivery and on how dyslexics actually think and learn. Much of the specialist dyslexia literature, though enlightening, seems to be written with PhD students in mind, in an arid and perplexing academic style that does not make good bedtime reading for an overworked teacher. Terms such as standard scores, working memory, processing speed and phonological awareness, applied liberally by Special Education Coordinators like me in Individual Education Plans, may be as difficult for chemistry teachers to get their head around as moles and hydrocarbons are for their pupils.

The lack of practical dyslexia know-how among many of our mainstream teachers percolates through into confusion, frustration, and sometimes anguish in the parents of dyslexic individuals. Without skillful, sensitive professional guidance, the discovery that your child has a learning disability can be a frightening, disorienting experience. Does this mean my child is dumb? What does it mean for his future career? How can I best support his homework? When should I be strict; when understanding? What does it mean when he comes home upset? Am I being too interfering in my engagement with his school? Or too laid back? Some parents commission an educational psychologist assessment but then struggle to understand the scores and terms used in the assessment report. Some find that they are explaining their child's learning profile and needs to his teachers over and over again at parent-teacher conferences. Many worry that, although they feel they understand their child, they don't feel they understand his dyslexia. Just as the hardworking dyslexic child is left with feelings of inadequacy after every class test, so his caring, dedicated parents are left feeling ineffectual when they sit down to help him with his homework.

This book is written for those who care about, and for, our struggling learners. To their teachers, it offers a solid, practical understanding of how they think, how they learn, and how they can succeed in our classrooms. Rather than being an encumbrance to a busy classroom teacher, dyslexic learners should be a litmus test: teaching that works for the dyslexic learner will enhance the learning of all. Dyslexic learners do not need a dumbed-down form of education; rather, they need to be taken more deeply and more immediately into the meaning of what they are learning, in ways that fully engage their faculties and capture their imagination. Once we start to understand how dyslexics think, our dyslexic learners can start to educate the educators.

To their parents, this book offers answers. It offers a support framework for their child's learning. It offers a common platform across which willing, informed parents can engage with willing, informed teachers in a joined-up approach to their children's education.

Like good teaching, this book aims to be as complicated as necessary, but as simple as possible. It aims to combine academic rigor with a plain-speaking, readable style. It aims to make sense.

A note on terminology: This book refers consistently to 'dyslexics' rather than to 'people with dyslexia'. This is done in full awareness that the latter is the more politically correct term; however, it risks framing dyslexia as something that 'happens' to someone, rather than an intrinsic part of a person's identity. This book promotes with passion the idea that dyslexia is not an affliction or disease, but rather a way of thinking, and therefore of learning. The intentional use of the term 'dyslexics' seems an appropriate way to celebrate this new paradigm.

Part I – Why *Tyrannosaurus* But Not *If*?

Chapter 1: 'I Don't Understand It – He Can Read *Tyrannosaurus* But He Gets Stuck On *If*!'

A number of years ago, a fellow dyslexia practitioner told me of a conversation she had had with a seven-year-old dyslexic boy whose parents had brought him to her for a first consultation.

'I know how to spell 'elephant'!' the boy had suddenly, spontaneously blurted out with considerable pride.

'Really? Tell me,' my associate replied.

'B-E-C-A-U-S-E'

If you are involved in primary education, you will know what had happened here. A common way of teaching the spelling of *because* is via an acronym: '*Big Elephants Cannot Always Use Small Exits.*'

This boy's misunderstanding of the lesson objective illustrates a crucial point. As with many dyslexics, this boy was a visual thinker. He learnt with and through his imagination. Pictures played a more important role in his thinking processes than did words. He probably had little awareness of the relationship between letters and their sounds. So when the teacher's acronym caused him to imagine an elephant, *B-E-C-A-U-S-E* became the spelling of the word that fitted his mental image.

The reasons why the mind of an imaginative, picture-thinking child may be more drawn to the word *elephant* than to the word *because* can show us a great deal about the nature and origins of the commonest of reading and writing difficulties. Consider this passage of text, from which some of the words have been blanked out:

_____ _____ for a _____. The ____ was _____ very _____, on the ___ at _____. Her ____ _____ was: would her ____ ____ to it? She was _____ of _____ him: he was quite a _____ _____

Put the first version out of your mind. Now here is another version, with different blanks:

Amelia thought ___ __ moment. ____ idea ___ certainly _____ attractive, ___ ___ surface __ least. ___ only hesitation ____: _____ ___ boss agree __ __? ___ ___ terrified _ asking ___: __ __ ___ _ formidable character.

In the first version, 22 words are shown and 16 are blanked out. In the second version, only 16 words are shown and 22 are blanked out. Why was the first version so much more difficult to understand than the second, even though it had fewer gaps?

'I DON'T UNDERSTAND IT – HE CAN READ TYRANNOSAURUS BUT HE GETS STUCK ON IF!'

The 16 words blanked out in the first passage (and shown in the second passage) are 'picture words' denoting objects, qualities and actions that the imagination easily engages with. Grammatically, picture words tend to include nouns, adjectives, most verbs and most adverbs.

By contrast, the 22 words shown in the first passage (and blanked out in the second passage) are 'connectives'. These words show us how to *arrange* the objects and events in our mental map. Is the cup *on* the table or *under* the table? Did I go out *because* it was raining or *although* it was raining? We can only 'see' the meaning of these words in the context of a whole phrase, clause or sentence; taken in isolation, these words do not normally evoke a mental image. Grammatically, connectives tend to be articles, prepositions, conjunctions, some adverbs, and certain auxiliary and modal verbs such as *have*, *will*, *must* etc.

Dyslexic readers tend to make frequent errors on connectives, even though they are some of the most common words in the English language and many are short words which 'should' be easy to recognize and pronounce. I have spoken with many parents and teachers who have observed this phenomenon in their dyslexic children or pupils. One mother's words stuck in my mind and sparked the title of this book:

'I don't understand it: he can read tyrannosaurus, *but he gets stuck on* if!'

Here is an extract from a reading error analysis I once undertook with a fourteen-year-old boy. While he was reading, I annotated my own copy of the text with 'h' for hesitations, 'o' for omissions and 'c' for self-corrections:

> By lunchtime I felt really upset and was missing all my friends at my old school, and Maria. I remember sitting down on the grass under a large shady tree and wondering what they were all up to. Fortunately though a boy from my class came over, and we got chatting. His name was Toby, and he was quite small with short dark hair and had a habit of staring open mouthed at things occasionally, but he was harmless and he was a good listener. We talked about many things, such as my old school, the girls there, the girls here, where my new house was and how well we were settling in, the girls who lived round about me, the weather, the most popular places to hang out at the weekends and where you had the most chance of seeing the girls...I noticed for the first time that teenage boys

From: Tiberius Goes to Rome (Peter A. Kay)

The high incidence of errors on connectives is striking. Given the curious nature of this phenomenon, it is remarkable that little serious research has been undertaken into it. This reader stumbled on words such as *had*, which is phonetically regular, consists of just three letters and makes up 0.25% of all words encountered in English-language books. By contrast, he read fluently a number of longer words, such as *fortunately* – a longer and phonetically more complex word which makes up just 0.0002% of words to be found in print in English.[1]

One way or another, innumerable observations of struggling readers suggest that the dyslexic mind retains and recognizes picture words much more readily than connectives. Many people familiar with dyslexia – as dyslexic individuals, as parents, as teachers, or as specialists – concur that dyslexics tend to have vivid, visual imaginations. It could well be asserted that imagination is a dyslexic's principal learning tool, which is another way of saying that the dyslexic mind craves *meaning* that can be *pictured*.

However, dyslexia is a field in which the 'common sense' observations of experienced specialists are not considered sufficient without the backing of an empirical evidence base – and probably rightly so, given the passion with which competing theories about the origins of the condition are promoted by their respective advocates. Readers of this book are given fair warning that it contains a blend: of reasoned propositions based on the author's and his colleagues' own experience in the field on the one hand; and of academic citations and research overviews on the other. While I shall attempt to hold these two ingredients in graceful balance, readers with a particular interest in the one should feel free to skim through sections dealing with the other. Books belong to

---

[1] (Google Books Ngram Viewer)

their readers as much, if not more, than they do to their author.

Research into dyslexia and visual abilities is still scant. Nonetheless, there is emerging evidence that dyslexia and a vivid visual imagination often correlate. Schurz et al[2] found that dyslexic subjects had heightened brain connectivity in the precuneus, an area of the brain associated with artistic[3] and visual[4] ability. Kramer[5] found that participants who are dyslexic have a tendency or preference to think with pictures of concepts and ideas versus internal dialogue. Von Károlyi and Winner[6] cite a range of evidence suggesting that people with reading and language problems are more highly represented among artists, mathematicians, inventors, and children exhibiting spatial strengths than they are in the general population.

The time-consuming nature of this kind of investigative research is probably the reason why the sample sizes in the above studies were all relatively small. Arguably, the quickest way to find out how large numbers of people think is to ask them. This is what the campaigning charity *Dyslexic Advantage* did, by conducting a survey of the thinking strengths of nearly 1100 individuals in 2015[7]. The most striking contrast

---

[2] (Schurz, et al., 2015)
[3] (Chamberlain, et al., 2014)
[4] (Cavanna & Trimble, 2006)
[5] (Kramer, 2016)
[6] (von Károlyi & Winner, 2004)
[7] (Dyslexic Advantage, 2015)

between dyslexic and non-dyslexic respondents is to be found in their responses to the statement: *'When I think through a problem, my thinking is more non-verbal (visual images, other sensory images, movements, etc.) than verbal (words).'* 80% of dyslexic respondents identified with the statement, compared with a mere 10% of non-dyslexic respondents. What are the implications of this marked contrast between the dyslexic 'picture-thinker' and the non-dyslexic 'word-thinker' – especially for anybody who has to teach a class containing pupils from both groups?

A crucial implication lies in the differences between how dyslexics and non-dyslexics can learn to read. According to Ronald D. Davis, author of *The Gift of Dyslexia* and *The Gift of Learning*, every word has three parts: what it looks like (i.e. its spelling), what it sounds like, and what it means. Conventional literacy teaching tends to focus on two of those three parts. Much reading instruction is based on a set of methods known collectively as phonics – an approach that links spelling to sound but ignores meaning. However, because dyslexic thinkers learn with and through their imagination, the third part of a word – what it means – is essential to how a dyslexic thinker will internalize and retain the word. It is the *meaning* of a word that transcends word-based thinking and engages directly with the imagination.

The Three Parts of a Word

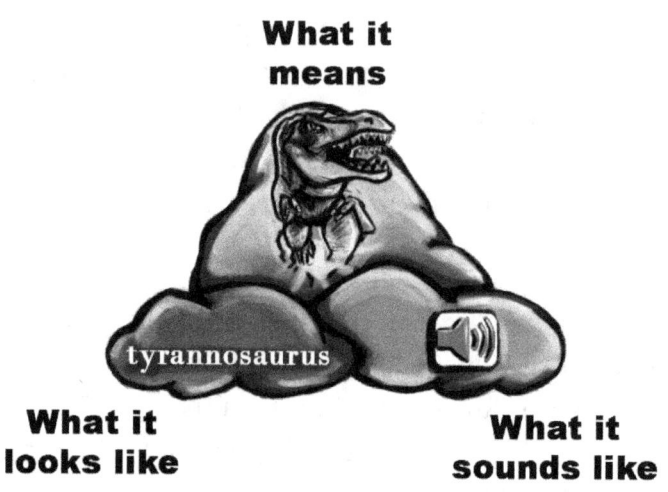

Figure 1: The three parts of a word

Phonic instruction is designed to link the bottom two parts of the above word triangle. First, a child learning to read is trained in *grapheme-phoneme correspondence,* which is the ability to link a letter with a speech sound. Some ardently pro-phonic schools initially teach children just the sounds of letters and not their names, storing up the unnecessary challenge of reprocessing each letter's identity later on when their actual names are introduced – rather like the confusion that you experience when a teacher whom you have known as 'Miss Smith' for three years gets married and you now have to remember to call her 'Mrs Jones', but multiplied 26 times over.

Then, a child is taught *blending*, the ability to draw individual sounds together to produce a word – e.g. realizing that the sounds *c-ă-t* make the word 'cat' – and *segmenting*, the reverse process of splitting a word into its phonemes and thence deducing the word's spelling[8] (this only works, of course, when the word is phonetically regular, so the numerous exceptions such as *–ough* words have to be taught separately).

When the instruction is successfully assimilated, the result is the ability to *decode*, meaning that a reader can deduce the sound of a word from its appearance on the page, without going via its meaning to get there. In the UK, six-year-olds are now tested on this specific skill by means of a reading test that includes so-called 'non-words': made-up combinations such as *koob* and *zort* that have no meaning and therefore can *only* be decoded phonically.[9] In the USA, many first-graders are similarly tested with the nonsense word subtest of the DIBELS suite.

We will look more closely at the benefits and limitations of phonic reading instruction for the general population in Chapters 4 and 5. For now, what is important is that the majority of children seem to find phonics an efficient vehicle for learning to read, but

---

[8] (National Literacy Trust)
[9] (Ward, 2010)

studies into phonic interventions tend to identify a significant minority who do not. One notable example in the UK was the North Yorkshire Reading Intervention, which was cited by Sir Jim Rose in a review of dyslexia and literacy support commissioned by the British Government[10] as evidence for the efficacy of synthetic phonics, despite the fact that 28% of children included in the intervention study did not progress. According to the authors, 'Definitions of dyslexia acknowledge that for a minority of children, reading problems are severe and persistent and response even to effective, well-implemented intervention is poor.'[11] Translated into plain-speak: some kids just can't learn to read, so it's not our fault that we couldn't help them.

In other studies, the rate of non-response to phonic intervention is still higher. For instance, another UK study by Savage, Carless and Erten into a Year 1 phonics intervention, delivered by experienced classroom aides to children at risk of reading problems, indicated that of the 74 children involved, 49 responded to the intervention and 25 did not.[12] Given the current evidence base, it is difficult to comprehend why both Sir Jim Rose and the UK Government should conclude that synthetic phonics are the appropriate method of instruction for all children and, essentially, instruct the UK educational establishment to stop looking for other teaching methods

---

[10] (Rose, 2009)
[11] (Centre for Reading and Language, 2009)
[12] (Savage, Carless, & Erten, 2009)

for the significant minority of children who persistently fail at this approach.

In fact, there is evidence to suggest that dyslexic individuals who learn effective reading strategies do so via a very different cognitive route to non-dyslexics. In her article, 'Brain Scans Show Dyslexics Read Better with Alternative Strategies'[13], Abigail Marshall cites studies by Rumsey and Horwitz and by Shaywitz et al, which indicate that dyslexics who have acquired effective reading skills show quite different patterns of brain activity to non-dyslexics when reading. These patterns involve greater right-brain activity than those apparent in non-dyslexics. By contrast, dyslexics who continue to *struggle* with reading show *similar* patterns of brain activity to the non-dyslexics. According to Marshall, 'This research suggests that for dyslexic readers, the left brain areas associated with phonetic decoding are ineffective. While a non-dyslexic reader finds such pathways an efficient route to reading, the dyslexic reader essentially becomes entangled in a neural traffic jam. In contrast, dyslexics who by-pass these mental pathways, relying more on areas of the brain involved in nonverbal thought and in analytic thought, are able to become capable readers.'

---

[13] (Marshall, 2003)

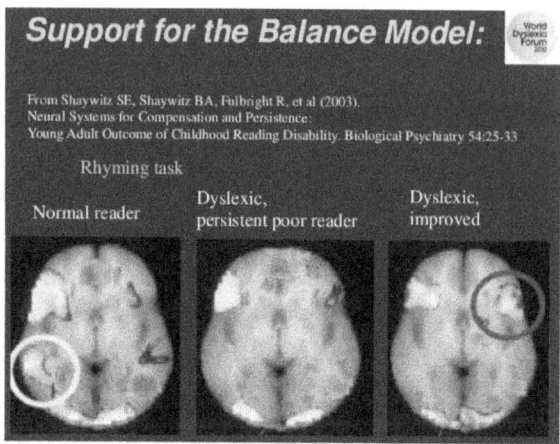

Figure 2: Shaywitz' research into dyslexic and non-dyslexic brain activity during reading. Source: Dr Maria Luisa Lorusso

Marshall's analysis of Shaywitz et al fits well with the so-called 'Dual-Route' hypothesis of reading fluency that has been proposed, in a number of variants, by a whole raft of psychologists, linguists and neurologists over the past century. For those readers who wish to dig deeper – a lot deeper – into the newer models based on this hypothesis, Coltheart et al's 'Dual Route Cascaded Model'[14] presents a detailed analysis of how a fluent reader could draw on both an inner 'lexicon' that links the spelling of a word directly to its meaning, and a grapheme-phoneme rule system providing a link from a word's spelling directly to its sound. According to the authors, an intricate system of 'inhibitory' and 'excitatory' connections directs fluent readers down the correct route – a little like a top-of-the-range Satnav, perhaps, that

---

[14] (Coltheart, et al., 2001)

knows all the possible routes as well as any roadworks and traffic jams along the way – enabling them to read both phonologically irregular words (such as *chef*) and non-words (such as *zort*) with equal prowess.

Pulling together the available evidence, we can construct a simple working model to show what the differences between dyslexic and non-dyslexic reading competency probably involve. Conventional, non-dyslexic readers who have responded well to phonic reading instruction have probably made a strong cognitive link between what the word looks like on the page and what it sounds like. Their internal experience of reading becomes a 'voice in the head' which is 'speaking' the words they are seeing. Provided they pay attention to this internal voice, and they are familiar with the vocabulary being used in the text, they will most likely comprehend what they are reading, possibly as whole phrases at a time. However, if they have a tendency to daydream, their attention is free to wander as the 'voice' reads on – so they may get to the end of a paragraph or page and realize they have understood little of what they have just read. As their primary cognitive route is from what the word looks like to what it sounds like, and only thence to what it means, they will do well in non-word reading tests and will most likely encounter no greater difficulty with connectives such as *if* than with picture words such as *tyrannosaurus*. A model of their experience of reading might resemble the illustration shown in Fig. 3:

The Three Parts of a Word

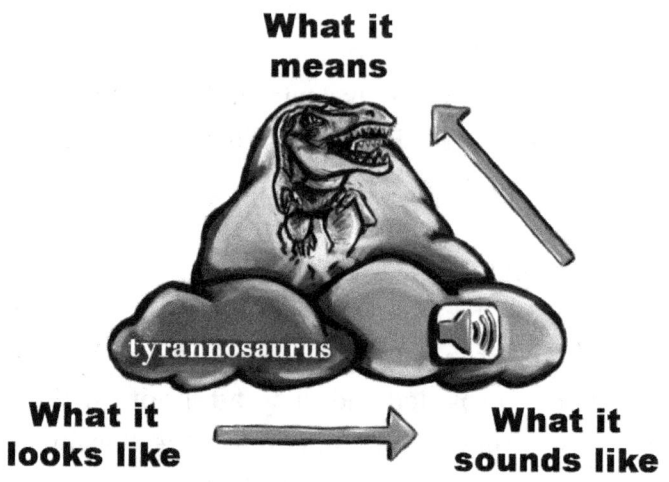

Figure 3: A phonic responder's route in reading

By contrast, those who are nearer the dyslexic end of the thinking spectrum will tend to engage in a very different process when reading. They will form a direct cognitive link from what words look like to what they *mean*. Their minds use the link to meaning to store the word so that it is recognized the next time it is encountered. The meaning of the word is experienced as a mental image. When required to read out loud, they will most likely go from the word on the page to their mental image of its meaning and only thence to its sound, as illustrated in Fig. 4:

The Three Parts of a Word

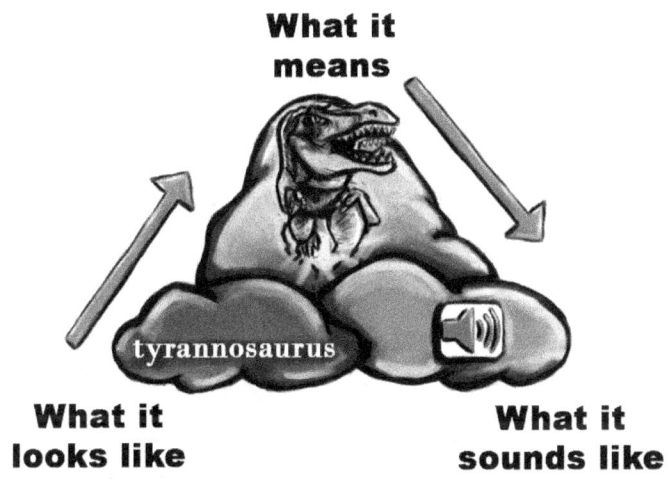

Figure 4: The typical dyslexic route in reading

However, this process will occur so quickly that an outside observer – or, for that matter, the dyslexic reader himself – will not usually be able to tell that the link from the written word to its sound is not direct. This only becomes clear when the meaning cannot be 'pictured': this will either block the reader completely, or force him to bypass the block by resorting to phonic strategies that do not come naturally to him. That is why this type of reader will tend to perform worse when reading non-words, abstract connectives such as *if*, and words outside of his existing vocabulary, than on picture words such as *tyrannosaurus* or *lilies*. A model of the problem might resemble the illustration shown in Fig. 5:

The Three Parts of a Word

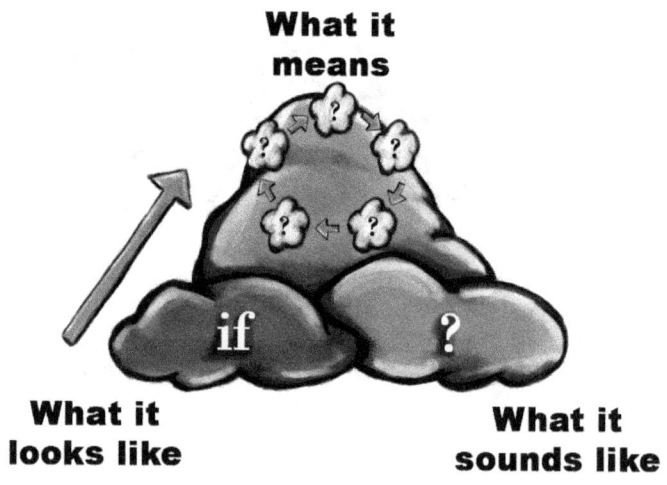

Figure 5: *The block that typically confronts a dyslexic reader when a word's meaning does not evoke a mental image*

Laying the problem out graphically reveals two different possible solutions. One logical route might be to continue exploring ways to train the dyslexic mind to go straight along the bottom of the triangle and get directly from what a word looks like to what it sounds like. This is the route taken by educationalists who believe that a child who is failing to learn to read through phonic teaching methods needs... well, more phonic teaching. However, as we have seen, while this approach may produce results for some struggling readers, there is a significant population of phonic non-responders for whom this approach does not work at all.

The other route, though equally obvious, rarely seems to feature in conventional educational models. If the problem with the common connectives is the lack of a mental image for the word's meaning, why not find a way for the student to fill the blank in? After all, these words *have* meaning, even if their purpose is to express a connection. In fact, the meaning of the small, common, abstract connecting words can hold profound lessons for a young learner.

Take the meaning of the word *because*. It is the law of cause and effect – a fundamental principle of Newtonian physics and of our understanding both of the material universe and of human interaction. Why would we want to exclude the meaning of *because* when we teach the word? Why on earth do we resort to acronyms involving big elephants and small exits *in preference* to engaging with this word's meaning?

> A story was relayed to me about an associate who, like me, is a Davis Dyslexia Program Facilitator. She was working through a Davis Program with a young dyslexic boy. On one day of the program, the boy became very upset because she refused to play a game with him until he had finished his model.
>
> Bemoaning this fact, he said, 'But you said we could play a game before lunch.' My associate's reply was, 'I said we could play a game before lunch *if* you had finished your model.'
>
> At this point, she realized that he didn't fully understand the meaning of the word *if*. Therefore, it seemed to him that she hadn't kept to her side of the bargain.

In secondary education and beyond, there are many individuals who have learnt to *memorize*, but not to *comprehend*: students who, on the eve of their high school diploma in Chemistry and after many years of teaching, have still not grasped the difference between electrons, protons and neutrons and barely understand the concept of an atom, let alone a molecule; adults with higher education degrees who think that the seasons occur because the earth travels further away from the sun in the winter and closer to it in the summer; destitute individuals who spend the 'same' money twice, because they never fully grasped the concept of subtraction, and then have no money left to pay their rent.

The irony is that many of the most vulnerable learners in our educational system are visual-spatial learners who excel at processing meaning, but whose vivid mental imagery so often remains dormant in an approach to education that is far too firmly rooted in the auditory and the phonic. There is an urgent need to widen the scope of our educational methods to embrace the needs of these learners, and there is a likelihood that *all* learners will find the resulting visual-spatial pageant of meaning exciting and stimulating. This book examines how this can be done – how education can become more memor*able* and less memor*ized*.

'If a child hasn't learnt, then I haven't taught; I have only attempted to teach. I then need to alter the way I attempt to teach – it could be by making alterations to the speed, the method, the environment or some other factor. I always try to change what I do – I cannot alter the child but I can influence the way he reacts.'

Caroline Smith,
Primary Special Education Specialist and
Davis Dyslexia Facilitator

Chapter 2: Working Backward from the Later Years: Observations of a Secondary School Teacher

To assess the extent and nature of a problem, one has to start by observing its effects. A central purpose of school education must be to equip young people adequately for adulthood by the time they leave the system. For many young people, this purpose is clearly fulfilled. However, some young people indubitably leave school insufficiently equipped for life. Analyzing the knowledge, skills and behaviors of these individuals should give us some clues as to any further ways in which primary and secondary school education could meaningfully be enhanced.

In this chapter, I will share some observations and case studies from my eleven years teaching in various roles in secondary education. These roles have included mainstream classroom teaching, heading up subject departments, one-on-one special education teaching and coordinating a Special Education department.

All my experience has been in the UK independent boarding sector, in environments where pastoral care is optimal, the teacher-student ratio high, and the extent and scope of contact between teachers and students greater than in most schools. In addition to teaching lessons, boarding school teachers have a wide range of other connections to their pupils: they typically eat lunch with them on an almost daily basis; they mentor pupils in small groups as an Academic Tutor; they run sporting and other co-curricular activities; and they supervise pupils in their boarding house through their evening routine of supper, homework, leisure time and bedtime. The issues cited in this chapter have all occurred *despite* the existence of excellent support structures at all levels. As we shall see in later chapters, the source of these issues is likely to lie at a much deeper level.

At one time, my role included the coordination of a team of teachers of the Theory of Knowledge course taken by all students of the International Baccalaureate (IB) Diploma. The course is assessed by means of a presentation given by each student to the whole class and an essay written on one out of a choice of six titles. As course coordinator, one of my responsibilities was to ensure that all students completed the essay in good time for the IB hand-in deadline. Coordinating student deadlines is insightful, because one gets to see how students have learnt to manage their time. The usual pattern is that some 80% of students hand their work in punctually, while the rest need to be chased to a greater or lesser extent. There is nothing out of the ordinary about this – most people need to be reminded of deadlines from time to time – but occasionally, the process goes to extremes.

One particular student – though this is not his real name, let us call him George – was taught by me during the first year of this two-year course and always struck me as intelligent and engaged: his written work, though a little brief, was of a good standard, and his participation in classroom discussion was excellent and astute. During the second and final year, however, it became difficult to get George to produce the presentation and essay which, if not submitted, would cost him his entire Diploma. His class presentation had to be rescheduled because he did not attend lessons on the day in question, complaining to the staff in his boarding house that he did not feel well. Even more crucially, he missed the hand-in deadline for the first draft of his essay, and his supervisor found it extraordinarily difficult to extract it from him. George assured his supervisor that it had been written, that he had actually already emailed it to him several times, that he could print out a hard copy for him shortly, that he could not do so just yet because of a technical failure on his computer.

This cycle continued until, with just three days remaining to the IB submission deadline, I asked for an urgent meeting with George. His boarding house staff found him sitting in the dark in his bedroom, looking extremely depressed and muttering that he was going to fail his Diploma.

Once I finally got to see George, he told me how he felt he was no good at Theory of Knowledge and had a complete mental block whenever he attempted to start the essay. Once he had owned up to the problem, I asked him a series of open-ended questions about the essay title until his thought process was in flow, showed him how to assemble his ideas in a mind map, then left him to get on with the essay in a distraction-free classroom, checking in with him every two hours or so as to his progress. He came to this classroom after lessons each day, and after three days, just in time for the deadline, he had a complete essay and ultimately achieved a respectable B-grade for the course.

From a purely rational point of view, George's behavior seems absurd. Despite being an able student in the subject, he had succumbed to a distorted view of his own abilities, feeling that nothing he produced could ever be good enough. Rather than seek support from his designated supervisor, he had hidden the problem away with a string of fabricated excuses, thereby placing his entire school-leaving qualification in jeopardy. He had followed the same pattern with his oral presentation, feigning illness to avoid delivering it and ultimately giving a rushed presentation just before the deadline. If perpetuated into adulthood, this pattern could cost an able student his university degree and prevent him holding down any but the most low-paid jobs involving minimal levels of responsibility.

One swallow does not make a summer, and a single anecdote is not yet evidence of a pattern. However, this is not really a single anecdote. Most secondary school teachers reading this book will be able to find similar examples among their students. While George's behavior was particularly extreme, I could have cited many more cases of students who underperform in relation to their ability because, for whatever combination of reasons, they fail to acquire the working habits and/or attitudes necessary for success.

Another pattern that I have observed is perhaps still more tragic. There are certain students who are extremely conscientious in their approach to their work and yet habitually underperform in tests or examinations. Despite meticulous preparation, these students find that they cannot recall their knowledge in a formal examination. Over time, this causes them to question, not just their ability, but the very processes by which their mind works. This tends to impact on their self-esteem and produce heightened anxiety in an examination, which in some cases can reach the level of panic attacks.

In many cases, these students have a profile of mild special educational needs. Their superb work ethic will mask this profile for a good while, so it may be detected late in their education. In the UK, this typically occurs in Year 10 (equivalent in age to Freshman year), when the build-up to the Year 11 GCSE qualification causes a shift of emphasis towards regular formal testing. Once detected, the student's cognitive profile will probably include restricted working memory. More will be said about working memory in Chapter 7; for now, a simple definition would be the mental 'workspace' a person has available to store multiple pieces of information in the short-term memory, manipulate them, and make something new out of them. Restrictions on working memory tend to accompany difficulties with mental arithmetic. Students with working memory restrictions will have problems with 'chalk-and-talk' lessons that are weighted towards information delivered orally by the teacher with little reinforcement through interactive or group exercises. They may find the information interesting at the time, but they will have little recollection of what was taught even a short time afterwards.

A good example of this phenomenon is a female Year 10 (Ninth Grade) student who was referred to me for one-to-one special education teaching because of examination anxiety. Although this is not her actual name, we will call her Jane. Initially, the brief was simply to explore relaxation techniques to alleviate her intense worrying. As we did so, it became apparent that Jane had no trust in her ability to retain factual information for tests, and this was the primary cause of her worry. On further probing, it emerged that she was using mainly *auditory* revision methods: she would look through a section of a book, sometimes writing her own notes, then attempt to recite the information to herself mentally.

However, she was an able sportswoman, and as we worked together it quickly became evident that her natural thinking strengths were *visual-spatial* and *tactile-kinesthetic* – she learnt best by *seeing* and *doing*.

Once we knew this, we were able to build a set of revision techniques for her which she quickly found to be effective. These might broadly be described as multisensory learning, but there is a crucial point to be made here. Traditionally, multisensory learning is sometimes restricted to reproducing the words in a text in a more visual way – using multi-colored highlighters, for instance, recreating the page in poster layout, or producing a mind map containing just words. However, as we have seen in Chapter 1, this type of learner craves *meaning*. We therefore started with a simple reading technique drawn from the Davis methods, about which more will be said in Part II of this book. Known as *Picture-At-Punctuation*, it involves pausing at punctuation marks (full stops, colons, semi-colons, some commas, etc.) to check if one can visualize or maybe 'feel' the meaning of the sentence or clause that has just been read.

With Jane, the results were striking in two ways. In subjects where she felt confident, the process of visualizing each clause or sentence improved her retention dramatically. Instead of trying vainly to internalize a huge number of word symbols, at the end of each section of her textbook she now had a gallery of mental images in her mind. These were the product of her own imagination, so she found it easy to retain them.

They linked precisely into the meaning of what she had read, so she could use them to recall the factual information she had read – accurately, and in considerable detail. She found this exciting.

In subjects where she was struggling, however, a very different pattern emerged. Applying the technique to the first sentence of a Chemistry revision guide, we found that she was unable to make a mental image of the following sentence:

'Atoms consist of three basic particles: electrons, protons and neutrons'.

At this point, the technique became diagnostic: it revealed that she had no mental image for the concepts of *atom*, *electron*, *proton* and *neutron*. Even the concept of *particle* was not entirely clear in her mind. We therefore used a combination of a dictionary and Google images until she could visualize these concepts; when we returned to the sentence in question, she could now visualize its meaning. Somewhat painstakingly, we continued through the first chapter in the same way, dealing with further concepts such as *element*, *mass*, *charge*, *atomic mass*, *atomic number* and *isotope* until she had a firm grasp of basic atomic theory.

The implications of this are sobering. A host of other concepts in Chemistry – covalent and ionic bonding, molecules, moles, ions and electrolysis to name but a few – will make no sense to a student who has not grasped basic atomic theory. For years of her education, Jane had internalized the lesson that academic success is just about hard work and rote-learning, whereas what she really needed was to *understand* – and for a long time, nobody around her had noticed that, in some of her core subjects, this need was not being fulfilled. This is by no means an isolated case; I have seen similar patterns in many pupils of similar age, especially (but by no means exclusively) in those with learning disabilities.

> About a year ago, I gave a presentation to a group of fellow special education teachers at which I emphasized how important it is for dyslexic learners to picture the meaning of what they are learning. Following the presentation, one colleague decided to try out a more visual approach when helping a 15-year-old pupil to understand acids and bases in Chemistry. As part of this approach, she asked the pupil to make a poster showing the color changes that occur in Universal Indicator at different stages of the pH scale. The pupil stated that, two years earlier, she had learnt that weak bases turn Universal Indicator indigo. When she started to create that part of the poster, however, she had a sudden realization: 'I don't actually know what indigo looks like!' At the age of thirteen, she had memorized a fact. Two years later, she understood it.

Effective revision can be summarized as a simple, three-step process:

Assimilation – Storage – Retrieval.

The reading technique of *Picture-At-Punctuation* had given Jane an effective process for *assimilation*. The next step was to give her a *storage* mechanism – in other words, to explore effective note-taking. The first principle we explored was that notes should not be a complete regurgitation of the words on the page of the textbook; rather, they should be a series of simple 'triggers' that, when reviewed before a test, bring back into the mind the gallery of mental images created when the page was originally read.

Jane found that mind maps were effective for this purpose. Mind maps are a visual-spatial way of laying out information or ideas; as such, they can be a useful vehicle both for planning one's own writing and for taking revision notes. Jane drew out her mind maps on paper, but by way of an example, here is an electronic mind map on the digestive process (the images were sourced via Google images; no infringement of copyright is intended):

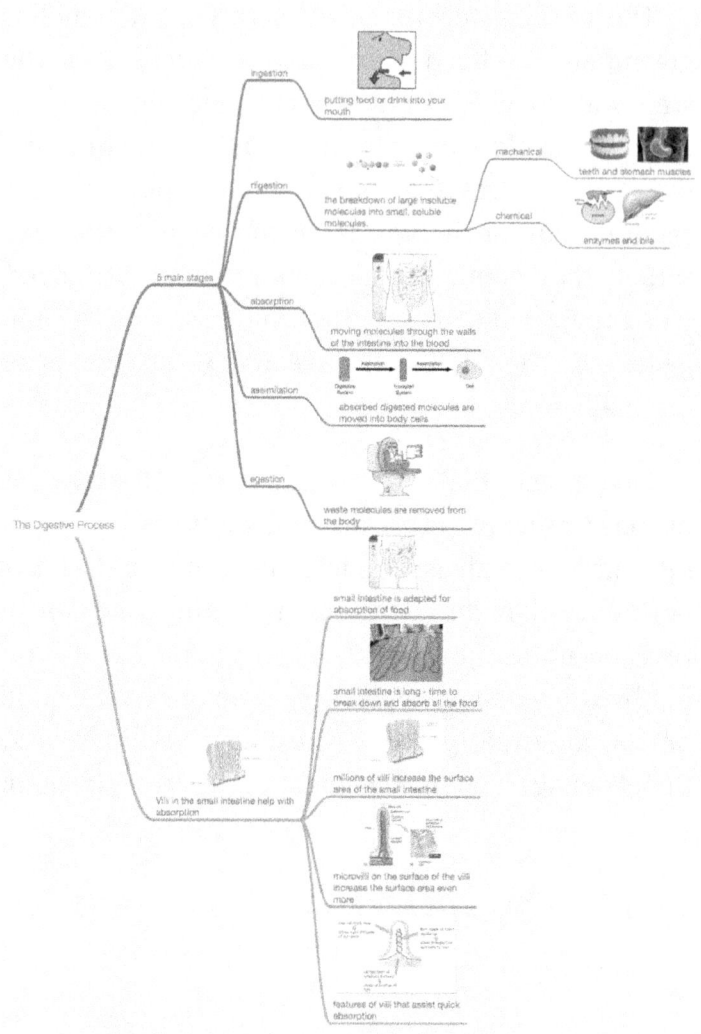

Figure 6: Example of an electronic mind map for subject revision

On the first mind map she produced, Jane learnt an interesting lesson. With each node of the mind map she created, I urged her to include, not just words, but a drawing or doodle depicting what the words *mean* – as was done in the electronic example above. However, she initially felt that this might be a waste of time, and so asked if she could leave the final two nodes with just words and no doodles. I then asked her to take a good look at her mind map, then close her eyes and see how much of it she could visualize. She had an immediate, striking realization.

Those areas where Jane had doodled in the meaning immediately presented themselves to her mind; what is more, her mental image of the doodle seemed to prompt or anchor the words, so she was able to retell their content to me fluently. By contrast, those areas where she had placed words but not doodles were a complete blind spot in her mental image: she had no recollection of them whatsoever. From then on, she required no further persuasion to include doodles in her mind maps and notes.

Once we had ensured that her *storage* mechanism was optimal, her *retrieval* sorted itself more or less automatically. For particularly challenging material, I showed her how to *assimilate* using the Davis Symbol Mastery® procedure, which works through the medium of reusable modeling clay. We did this for the reactivity series in Chemistry, for instance, prior to a class test. A few days later, I received this email from her:

> Dear Mr Whitehead,
>
> Hope 5:00 is still ok for tomorrow.
> I received my chemistry mark back and got 96% so VERY happy...
>
> Kind Regards

At our next lesson, she told me that, prior to this, she had never obtained more than 48% in any Chemistry test – ever.

In a sense, Jane, George and the many other students who exhibit similar patterns had been deflected from the key purpose that all school education should fulfil. The purpose of education must surely always be to *understand*. George had no difficulty conceptualizing the meaning of what he was being taught, but there were some key gaps in his understanding of *himself* that, for whatever reasons, had not been resolved over thirteen years of school education. Jane had worked so hard that, for years, nobody around her had detected that there were great voids in her understanding of key subject material. That which goes undetected goes unaddressed: Jane never realized the crucial difference between memorization and understanding until the intellectual demands of her education reached the point where the former started to fail her.

In February 2017, research by the BBC revealed that around twenty percent of pupils at UK independent secondary schools receive an additional time allowance of 25% or more to complete their high school public examinations.[15] The corresponding number of pupils at state schools is lower, but the UK examinations regulator Ofqual attributes this to the 'readiness' of independent schools to identify students in need – not to over-detection by these schools. To qualify for an additional time allowance, a student must have been assessed as significantly below average in speed of writing, reading (word recognition or comprehension), or in a cognitive domain. Additionally, the student needs to have demonstrated a history of need – simply put, the student needs to have struggled or failed to complete examination papers within the standard time allocated.

If Ofqual's interpretation is correct, and one fifth of teenagers are unable to demonstrate their full ability within the standard time allocated to a public examination, what are the implications of this for workflow and well-being in later life? How should we relate to these figures? Should we accept them as inevitable human variability, or should they impel us to reassess whether the education we are giving to our children is fully fit for purpose?

From all of this, two key questions arise. Given the lot of students such as Jane, should adjustments be made to the ways we educate children – adjustments that embed comprehension so firmly into *all* learning that it becomes impossible to mistake the difference between memorization and understanding? And for students such as George, could such adjustments lead to a deeper level

---

[15] (British Broadcasting Corporation, 2017)

of understanding of the world around us that, in turn, leads to an enhanced understanding of ourselves?

This will be the focal point of further chapters of this book. First, however, we need to consider some fundamentals about the thinking process itself.

Chapter 3: Words and Pictures: Verbal and Trans-Verbal Thinking

'...the development of speech and the development of consciousness... go hand in hand.' – Friedrich Nietzsche, *The Joyful Wisdom*.

'Take care of the sense, and the sounds will take care of themselves.' Lewis Carroll, *Alice in Wonderland* (spoken by the Duchess).

An underlying assumption of the current mainstream in literacy teaching is that reading can only be taught successfully through the medium of phonics. Phonics are an approach to reading teaching based on the correlations between written symbols and spoken sounds. To do the internal mental work to decode a word phonically, you have to have an 'inner voice': you have to be able to think with the sounds of words without speaking them out loud. It follows that many educators nowadays are assuming that children *have to* think with an inner voice in order to learn to read.

Thinking with an inner voice, or verbal thinking, is commonplace. I do it, and from numerous interactions with workshop participants and the audiences at my lectures and talks, it would seem to me that most adults do it. It is the mode of thinking which one might employ, for instance, when rehearsing a difficult conversation that one needs to hold with a relative or line manager, or when thinking about the exact words that one needs to compose an email or other written text.

The above quotation from Nietzsche exemplifies a pervading view in some philosophical circles that all conscious thinking is verbal thinking. At first sight, it may appear that leading thinkers in the field of language hold to this premise too. Ferdinand de Saussure was one of the most influential thinkers in the field of semiotics. A sub-domain of linguistics, semiotics is the study of signs and symbols (including words and language generally) and how as humans we use them. According to Saussure:

'Psychologically, our thought – apart from its expression in words – is only a shapeless and indistinct mass. Philosophers and linguists have always agreed in recognizing that without the help of signs we would be unable to make a clear, consistent distinction between two ideas. Without language, thought is a vague, uncharted nebula. There are no pre-existing ideas, and nothing is distinct before the appearance of language.'[16]

Looking at this quotation in isolation, it would be easy to infer that Saussure sees our intelligence and our ability to think with the sounds of words as one and the same. This would be a wrong and damning conclusion in respect of those dyslexic thinkers who frequently score at a low level in tests of phonological awareness, which essentially assess a person's ability to think with the sounds of words. According to the Rose Report, 'Characteristic features of dyslexia are difficulties in phonological awareness, verbal memory and verbal processing speed.'[17] It would be absurd to deduce from a combined reading of Rose and Saussure that the thoughts of Richard Branson, Thomas Edison, Richard Rogers and other patently talented dyslexics were 'a shapeless and indistinct mass'.

In reality, Saussure uses terms such as *signs*, *words* and *language* to refer to the interaction *between* thought and sound – a kind of filing system involving both sound and meaning that we develop in order to carve and categorize the physical and mental universes into distinct units. Drawing an example from the title of this book, we might illustrate Saussure's view by saying that a person's experience of the word *tyrannosaurus* will be both the sound of the word and the mental image associated with what it means. However, Saussure would go further and

---

[16] (de Saussure, [1916] 1959), pp. 111 – 112
[17] (Rose, 2009)

maintain, perhaps, that it is only through devising the word *tyrannosaurus* that we can perceive and categorize the difference between a tyrannosaurus and a diplodocus or a velociraptor.

Even with this deeper interpretation of Saussure's view, a core assumption remains that all intelligent and organized thought is dependent on language. Yet this assumption is called into question by everyday experiences such as these:

1. You are at a social function and suddenly realize that you forgot to turn off the iron at home;
2. You trip while walking down the stairs and grab the banister to steady yourself;
3. You meet someone and have a clear recollection that you have met them before, though you cannot recall their name;
4. You are assembling a flat-pack piece of furniture and have a small, nameless component left over in the bottom of the box after assembly. You suddenly realize where that component should have been placed;
5. You want to ask a family member to pass you a certain household object, but you can't recall its name, so you say, 'Pass the thingamajig.'

It would be far-fetched to maintain that any of the above *intelligent* thought processes had anything to do with *language*. Indeed, it would be a sorry state of affairs for humanity if our thinking processes derived *from* language. Common sense dictates that it must be the other way around. How else would our vocabulary ever grow? The colloquial verb *to frape* is defined by yourdictionary.com as: 'An act of using another person's Facebook account to post derogatory messages.' Yet the first person ever to be fraped must have been fraped at a time when the word *frape* did not yet exist. The experience or idea of fraping must have come first, after which the fraped, the frapers and the frape-arbitrators must have come up with a word symbol to discuss the act. However did we come up with the idea that the symbolic code we use to communicate with each other is also the epicenter of our ordered thinking? Is eloquence the same thing as intelligence? Are the chattiest people the cleverest? Do American football cheerleaders think in flags?

John Major, the beleaguered UK Prime Minister of the 1990s, inadvertently provided an exquisite clue to what intelligence actually is when he spoke to the media outside his Downing Street residence after a rout of his party in the 1995 local elections. He was asked if he was considering resigning, and he responded thus:[18]

'It is not in my mind. I have never run away from a difficulty in my life and I don't intend to do so now. And for those people who may suggest - and some have - that at the moment the Conservative Party has its backs to the wall, I would simply say, we will do precisely what the British nation has done all its history when it's had its

---

[18] (Associated Press, 1995)

back to the wall – that was, turn around and fight for the things it believes in – and that's what I shall do.'

Good phonic readers may miss the joke. The comical mental image of a Conservative leader in quixotic combat with a wall is precisely that: an image. We get the joke only when our thinking transcends the realm of words, signs and language and converts the text into an internal experience. Our phonological, lexical and syntactic knowledge are not enough: to engage intelligently with what was said, we need imagination.

Though we will shortly discuss why it is far more than this, mental imagery or imagination might loosely be described as 'picture thinking'. Professor Steven Pinker, a renowned contemporary writer on psychology and language, cites an intriguing picture-thinking experiment that he conducted together with fellow-psychologists Ronald Finke and Martha Farah on an unspecified number of subjects:

'Imagine the letter *D*. Rotate it 90 degrees to the right. Put the number 4 above it. Now remove the horizontal segment of the 4 to the right of the vertical line.

'Imagine the letter *B*. Rotate it 90 degrees to the left. Put a triangle directly below it having the same width and pointing down. Remove the horizontal line.

'Imagine the letter *K*. Place a square next to it on the left side. Put a circle inside the square. Now rotate the figure 90 degrees to the left.

'Most people had no trouble reporting the sailboat, the valentine, and the television set that were implicit in the verbiage.'[19]

Though the instructions were given through the medium of language, verbal thinking is useless as a tool for finding the answers. This is an intriguing experiment, as it confirms what many of the world's great thinkers claimed already to know: that internally generated mental imagery can be used to solve problems, in isolation from verbal processes. Anecdotal evidence of the intelligent use of mental imagery by innovative scientists abounds: Kekulé recounts how his theory of molecular constitution arose out of a 'reverie' in which he saw atoms 'gamboling before my eyes'; Faraday saw the stresses surrounding magnets and electric currents as curves in space; and then there is Einstein's famous quotation: 'The words of language, as they are written or spoken, do not seem to play any role in my mechanism of thought. The physical entities which seem to serve as elements in thought are certain signs and more or less clear images.'[20]

Of course, to suppose that all of our intelligence comes down to playing with images on a mental screen – a kind of internalized self-designed video game – would be to over-simplify the depth and complexity of human thought. Pinker again, despite recognizing the central and

---

[19] (Pinker, 1999), p. 293
[20] (Koestler, 1964), pp. 169 - 170

powerful role of mental imagery in our intelligence, states reservations:

'...How could a concrete image represent an abstract concept, like 'freedom'? The Statue of Liberty is already taken; presumably it is representing the concept 'the Statue of Liberty.' What would you use for negative concepts, like 'not a giraffe'? An image of a giraffe with a red diagonal line through it? Then what would represent the concept 'a giraffe with a red diagonal line through it'? How about disjunctive concepts, like 'either a cat or a bird,' or propositions, like 'All men are mortal'?

'Pictures are ambiguous, but thoughts, virtually by definition, cannot be ambiguous. Your common sense makes distinctions that pictures by themselves do not; therefore your common sense is not just a collection of pictures.'[21]

Somehow, the human mind seems able to combine mental imagery, experience, and perhaps a sprinkling of emotion to create a web of intelligence that is able to place each new experience instantly into an appropriate context, make both logical predictions and intuitive judgements, and develop the elusive trait that we call 'common sense'. The more mysterious elements of this process go beyond the scope of this book. What is important to us as educators is that there are substantial grounds for supposing that our imagination – encompassing not just visual imagery but all of the senses

---

[21] (Pinker, 1999), p. 297

– plays a central part in our intelligent processes. By contrast, the evidence that some form of internally 'spoken' word symbols plays a similarly pivotal role in our intelligence seems flimsy at best.

The use of visualization to turbo-charge comprehension is supported by a substantial body of research.[22] In the previous chapter, we saw how the Davis procedure, *Picture-At-Punctuation* (scripted in Part II of this book) can greatly increase retention of the content of a text by comparison with purely phonic methods of reading. I have worked with pupils who, by using this technique, could recall the content of a page of text in every detail two, and sometimes even three, weeks after initial reading, with no 'revision' of the material in the interim. In the previous chapter, we saw how Jane could visualize and retain mind maps that incorporated images far more easily than areas of her notes involving only words. I have observed the same effect with a number of other pupils whom I have worked with. Whether or not the mental image is the be all and end all of our thinking process is ultimately of greater interest to psychologists than to educators. The realization that mental imagery is far more essential to our thinking processes than are words, even if many of us tend to be more conscious of the latter than of the former, has significant implications for the education of all.

As we saw in Chapter 1, the grapheme-phoneme correspondence that sits at the heart of phonic reading

---

[22] (Davis Dyslexia Association International, 2012)

teaching assumes comprehension rather than exploring it. The presence or absence of a mental image for the meaning of common connectives such as *if*, *the*, *unless*, *because* etc. goes untested, despite the significance of these words for children's learning and the high incidence of error on them among dyslexics. In mathematics, we move from the manipulation of real quantities to the world of symbols too early, depriving some learners of a thorough understanding of processes such as *subtract*, *multiply* and/or *divide* and thereby allowing subtle lifelong difficulties to persist. Later, we talk to older children using terms such as *responsibility*, *justice*, *consequence* and *morality* without checking whether their understanding of these concepts is clear, and how similar or different their mental image for these words is to our own.

Dictionaries are an indispensable tool for clarifying the meanings of words, but they have their limitations. The Oxford Dictionary of English[23] defines *loyalty* as 'the quality of being loyal'. Looking up *loyal* delivers 'giving or showing firm and constant support or allegiance to a person or institution.' Looking up *allegiance* takes us back round to 'loyalty or commitment to a superior or to a group or cause.' Need I go on, or do you get the idea?

Dictionary definitions define words using other words. Using symbols to define symbols only works if one of the symbols we encounter provides an exit from this circular lexical highway by linking up with a mental image that

---

[23] (Oxford University Press)

correlates to a personal experience. The exit from word symbols into imagery is subtly unique for each individual reader, as it marks the point where meaning is extracted from the shared pool of language into the individual's unique gallery of mental images and experiences.

When the word being defined is a concrete concept such as *desk* or *walk*, it is likely that this subtle uniqueness is of little concern. Yet what about abstract words such as *loyalty*? In his account of the Second World War, Winston Churchill [24] states that the so-called *Knickebein* technology used by the German military in the autumn of 1940 to guide their bomber pilots to major UK cities through a combination of radio beams was intercepted, interfered with, and largely thwarted by radiologists working for the UK government. Churchill claims that, while the German air crews soon suspected that their beams were being 'mauled', nobody had the courage to tell Hermann Goering, who was in charge of the *Luftwaffe* and had absolute faith in the *Knickebein* project. According to Churchill, 'special lectures and warnings were delivered to the German Air Force, assuring them that the beam was infallible, and that anyone who cast doubt on it would be at once thrown out.' Under such circumstances, what would have constituted *loyalty* in a Luftwaffe pilot? Supporting Goering's view, or telling him the truth? If one of the pilots had followed the latter interpretation and Goering

---

[24] (Churchill, 1949), p. 343

the former, would a dictionary have spared the pilot from discharge or, perhaps, something more fatal?

Far more sinister examples of semantic contortions are all too easy to find in recent European history: Heinrich Himmler's praise for SS Group Leaders in his 1943 Posen Speech, whom he extolled for remaining 'decent' despite ordering and witnessing the execution of thousands of Jews[25]; Maxim Gorky's tribute to 13-year-old Pavlik Morozov's 'heroic action' in denouncing his own father Trofim to the Soviet secret police in 1932 for allegedly hoarding grain (Trofim was sent to a labor camp for 10 years and was executed while serving his sentence)[26]; Islamic State's more recent hijacking of the concept of *belonging* to recruit unwitting young westerners to their cause[27] – to name but a few. The lesson for us as educators should be obvious: how can we bolster our young against willful distortions of humanity's conceptual fabric that ultimately lead to their own physical and/or moral annihilation, let alone the damage or destruction wrought on others? How can we ensure that the young people entrusted to our care do not know these concepts as mere words, but are *experienced* in their understanding of what they mean?

The full implications of these questions go beyond the scope of this book. However, an approach to literacy teaching that utilizes experiential learning as a first resort

---

[25] (Gavin, 2015)
[26] (Rayfield, 2005)
[27] (Winter, 2015)

rather than a last resort creates a new precision in a learner's exploration of what words mean. This can be a useful supplement to more generalized approaches to critical thinking. Examples of how this can be achieved are to follow in Part II.

Chapter 4: To Sound or Not To Sound? That Is The Primary Question

In Chapter 1, we discussed how there are three parts to every word: what it looks like, what it sounds like, and what it means. Phonic-based literacy instruction was examined as an approach that builds the link between the appearance and sound of a word, assuming that a native speaker already grasps its meaning, but without explicitly assessing whether this is the case. We considered how this can be a sound approach for the majority of learners, but how children who are phonic non-responders, including those with dyslexia, tend to fail surprisingly on the small, abstract words of a language such as *if*, *the*, *but*, *when* etc. We discussed the clue that this failure gives us to the central role of meaning in the way that these children process and assimilate reading vocabulary.

It is time now to explore the wider implications of the choice to define reading as the decoding of written symbols into sound, rather than as the extraction of meaning from them. Sue Lyle, a part time Senior Lecturer at Swansea Metropolitan University in Wales and

Director of Dialogue Exchange Ltd., comments critically on this choice as follows:

'I can read Welsh, a language with very regular letter-sound correspondences, quite well, but the problem is, I don't understand any of it. I have taught many Muslim children who have learnt to decode the Koran, but they don't understand the Arabic they are reading. There is a world of difference between decoding and reading.'[28]

Proponents of phonic-based reading instruction can be evangelical in their insistence that success in reading can only ever be achieved through their methods. A contributor to the Special Education Coordinator email forum provided by the UK Department for Education put it thus: [29]

'...it strikes me as absurd to think of teaching reading without teaching phonics, since the whole reading system is based upon letters, or patterns of letters, representing sounds. It would be as crazy as teaching Math without explaining that the value of a digit alters according to its place in the number.

'...to use... the difficulty some children have to learn phonics as an excuse not to teach them is as crazy as saying it's hard for some children to learn to balance on a bike so we'll teach them to ride the bike some other way... there IS no other way!'

---

[28] (Lyle, 2014)
[29] (Kelly, 2015)

The zeal behind such utterances is understandable. The high emotions around this debate stem from what James Kim describes as 'the Reading Wars': a sometimes embittered conflict between proponents of phonic decoding and adherents to 'whole-word' methods based on the extraction and deduction of meaning.[30] Kim traces the hostilities back to the mid-nineteenth century, when the secretary of the Massachusetts Board of Education, Horace Mann, derogated the letters of the alphabet as 'bloodless, ghostly apparitions' and argued that children should first learn to read whole words. Through much of the twentieth century, and on both sides of the Atlantic, phonic educators looked on helplessly as the decoding methods with which they had successfully taught so many children were challenged, first by a repetitive 'look-say' approach which required children to commit vast numbers of whole words to visual memory, and later by psycholinguistic 'whole language' theories that emphasized contextual guess-work over accuracy of word recognition. When research evidence, such as that gathered by UK Local Education Authorities in the second half of the 1980s and collated by Martin Turner in his essay, 'Sponsored Reading Failure'[31], suggested that whole-language approaches had been responsible for alarming downward trends in reading proficiency, the political pendulum started to swing back towards phonics. Current policy in the UK, as laid down by the Coalition Government in 2012, requires all primary

---

[30] (Kim, 2008)
[31] (Turner, 1994)

teachers and trainee teachers to be proficient in synthetic phonics.

Understandably eager to protect future generations from past reading failure which they attributed to previous 'mixed method' approaches, a number of influential educators have been keen to fasten the political pendulum securely to the decoding side of the metaphorical literary clock. They advocate synthetic phonics as the only route to reading with an absolutist fervor of the kind that, when detected in a conversation partner at a social function, inclines one to feign an urgent interest in the bathroom facilities. The website dyslexics.org.uk, described by its owner and author Susan Godsland with a soupçon of sanctimony as an 'independent, fad-free and no-nonsense website', declaims on its homepage that 'synthetic phonics is the educational vaccine that protects children from illiteracy.'[32] Elsewhere on the site, with somewhat Maoist vigor, Godsland attacks university teacher training departments in general for providing their student teachers with 'subversive subtext and false balance' to ensure that synthetic phonics teaching is 'undermined'. The Reading Wars are anything but over: the lack of trust, constructive dialogue and, above all, professional respect between literacy experts in the different 'camps' is all the more tragic when one considers that the combatants belong to the very profession whom we trust to cultivate open-mindedness, analytical rigor, and a spirit of enquiry

---

[32] (Godsland)

in our own children. The more extreme antics of this futile conflict make a compelling case for home education.

A frequent casualty of any form of war is pluralism. In a major conflagration, it becomes difficult for small, civilized states caught amidst the combatants to maintain their neutrality without taking sides. The Reading Wars are no exception: they have polarized and trivialized the debate around reading instruction to the point where anyone who states reservations around 'phonics for all' must be a whole-word enthusiast, and vice versa. Other reading teaching strategies with good intellectual pedigree, strong success statistics, and an open system approach that allows for integration of the best elements of both phonic and whole-word teaching are denied their rightful place in the public literacy debate.

Take morphological approaches to reading, for example. A phoneme is the smallest unit of sound in a language – such as *k, ă* or *t* in the English word *cat*. A morpheme is the smallest unit of meaning in a language – such as *un-*, *-think-* or *able* in the word *unthinkable*. A growing body of academics feels that morphological teaching provides young readers with analytical tools that are a helpful supplement to their phonic and comprehension skills. Canadian researchers Kirby and Bowers cite a number of ways in which teachers have integrated morphological instruction into their teaching methods, reporting that children usually find the approach exciting:

- *Use a Word Detective approach:* After a morphological pattern has been taught, encourage students to search for examples in class texts.
- *Incorporate word sums and word matrices:* Present words that might be related by a base (e.g., *interrupt, corrupt, eruption*) Have students identify a common base and test their hypotheses using word sums (e.g., inter + rupt, cor + rupt, e + rupt). Then construct a word matrix around this base.
- *Collect data banks of morphemes:* Create a sticky note morpheme chart in the class, adding affixes and bases as you encounter them.
- *Use expository texts from a variety of subjects:* For example, in a lesson on condensation in science, address the 'density' of molecules in different states of matter. Use a word sum to identify the link in spelling and meaning between these words and their common base <dense> (con + dense/ + ate/ + ion condensation; dense/ + ity density).
- *Invite students to use a SMART Board:* This is good visual tool for matching morphemes with meanings and/or circling base words.
- *Have students create sets of color-coded morpheme cards:* Students can use one color for prefixes, another for suffixes. As new base words are introduced, have students create corresponding white cards, to use in conjunction with their affix cards.[33]

---

[33] (Kirby & Bowers, 2012)

The Maple Hayes Dyslexia School and Research Centre in Staffordshire, England takes an integrated morphological approach to literacy acquisition. The school's approach is explained in depth by its founder, Neville Brown, in his book, 'Meaning, Morphemes and Literacy'[34]. In its 2011 report on Maple Hayes, the UK's education inspectorate, Ofsted, commented thus:

'The curriculum is outstanding. The school has developed a unique, visual approach to teaching literacy skills as an alternative to the phonics approach which pupils have so far been unable to use effectively. The school's system breaks words down into segments of meaning which are then assigned pictorial icons. These help pupils to understand and read the words. The formation of correct handwriting is also heavily emphasized to reinforce reading and understanding. These specific skills are taught highly systematically. They are practiced in dedicated lessons and in special computer-based sessions, tested every week along with spelling, and reinforced throughout the curriculum. The overwhelming majority of pupils and their parents and carers are very pleased with this approach, and pupils say that they will always need and use this methodology. Numerous comments on inspection questionnaires say that Maple Hayes has transformed pupils' lives and future prospects.'[35]

---

[34] (Brown, 2009)
[35] (Charlesworth, 2011)

Despite this and plentiful other independent accolades, Maple Hayes School and its approach are not mentioned anywhere on the British Dyslexia Association website. On Susan Godsland's dyslexics.org.uk site, it is consigned, without explanation, to a page she entitles, 'Room 101: Fad, fraud and folly in 'dyslexia' and the teaching of reading.'

The British Dyslexia Association is unequivocal in placing phonic instruction at the center of all dyslexia specialist literacy tuition. 'Specialist literacy tuition,' it states, somewhat ungrammatically, 'is: 1. Phonic. 2. Structured. 3. Cumulative. 4. Multisensory. 5. Withdrawal or Inclusion? 6. The Alphabet.'[36] The International Dyslexia Association is similarly unreserved in its insistence on phonic remediation for dyslexia. Its *Structured Literacy* approach does advocate a blend of elements that include phonology, morphology, syntax and semantics, but it criticizes other reading approaches such as Guided Reading and Balanced Literacy as 'especially ineffective for students with dyslexia because they do not focus on the decoding skills these students need to succeed in reading'.[37]

Notwithstanding this unhesitating endorsement of 'phonics for all' by key dyslexia associations on both sides of the Atlantic, phonic approaches are problematic for many learners with special educational needs, especially when used in isolation. Phonics *do* work well for the

---

[36] (British Dyslexia Association, 2015)
[37] (International Dyslexia Association, 2015)

majority of young readers, and they quite rightly occupy a central place in mainstream reading teaching instruction. However, any sensibly differentiated approach to literacy teaching needs to be mindful of the needs of the following minority communities of learners:

1. Pupils with low phonological awareness. In lay terms, phonological awareness is the ability to identify and manipulate speech sounds (phonemes) internally. Because grapheme-phoneme correspondences are the starting point of phonic instruction, learners with low phonological awareness will, by definition, be handicapped in phonic approaches to reading: they will lack the cognitive apparatus to move along the bottom of the 'Three Parts of a Word' triangle with fluency and accuracy.

The Three Parts of a Word

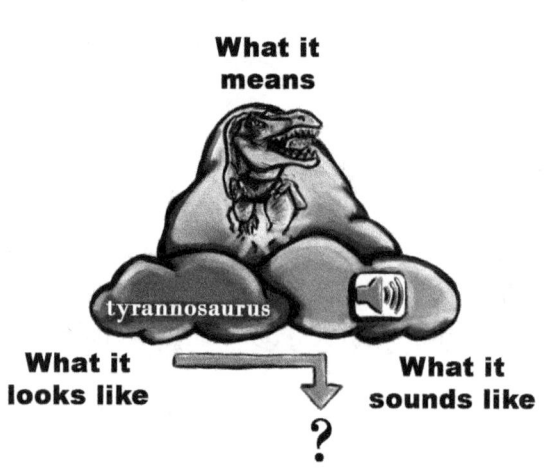

Figure 7: The problem with phonics for learners with low phonological awareness

2. Pupils with visual dyslexia. These are people who experience one or several of the following:

- Blurred letters or words which go out of focus.
- Letters which move or present with back to front appearance or shimmering or shaking.
- Headaches from reading.
- Words or letters which break into two and appear as double.
- Difficulty with tracking across the page.
- Upset by glare on the page or oversensitive to bright lights.[38]

These learners will not be helped by phonic instruction unless or until some form of remediation has been provided for the perceptual distortions that are making the letters seem to blur, flip, or change places. Phonics is a decoding strategy; it is not a recognition strategy. If the word and its component letters have not been discerned accurately in the first place, the hapless learner will be decoding a distorted mental image of the word and is doomed to failure.

---

[38] (British Dyslexia Association, 2015)

The Three Parts of a Word

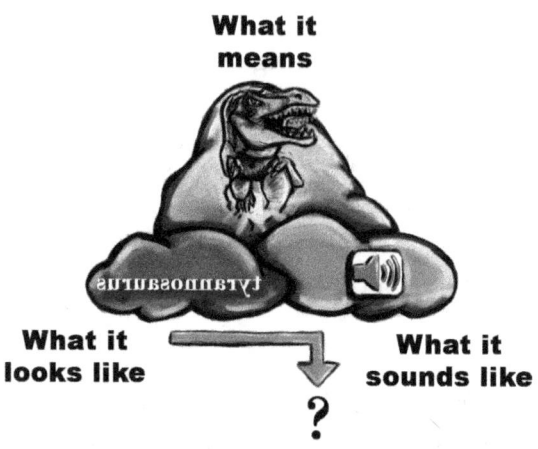

Figure 8: The problem with phonics for learners with visual dyslexia

3. Pupils with attention focus issues. I have encountered a number of such pupils who test with robust phonological awareness and who have responded *successfully* to phonic teaching instruction. Because of its emphasis on grapheme-phoneme correspondences, phonic teaching tends to produce readers who experience internal monologue. Combine this with a lively, wandering imagination, and you get a reader who becomes a victim of his own phonological success. Lulled into an automated process of moving from left to right along the bottom of the 'Three Parts of a Word' triangle, the reader's mind runs feral as it has not been rigorously trained in the necessary further job of paying attention to the meaning of what is being read. Such readers may need

to re-read the same paragraph several times in order to extract its meaning:

The Three Parts of a Word

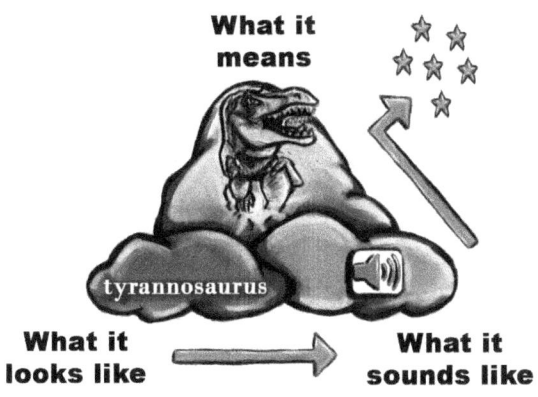

Figure 9: The problem with phonics for learners with attention focus issues

So can the Reading Wars ever reach an armistice? Amidst such a flurry of conflicting opinions on the way forward for literacy teaching, is it possible to find a unifying principle, an indisputable starting premise for the teaching of reading that phonic, whole-word, and all other reading methodologies will agree upon? Furthermore, could such a principle furnish an agreed conceptual foundation for reading teaching, around which we can configure a route map for literacy that deploys appropriate strategies at appropriate times for each learner?

This is the subject of the next chapter.

Chapter 5: What Reading Is

The previous chapter ended with a question: can a starting principle be identified that is *more fundamental* to the acquisition of reading skills than both grapheme-phoneme correspondences and whole-word theory?

Such a principle exists:

A word is written as a sequence of letters. It can be pronounced, and it carries meaning.

This qualifies as a unifying principle because it is the simplest universal, indisputable, and therefore non-ideological statement that can be made about the nature of words. Though not taken from a dictionary, it has the quality of a dictionary definition.

Crucially, it frees grapheme-phoneme correspondences from the burden of being the unifying principle. Phonic instructors felt that they had to fulfil that role, because the competing option – whole-word recognition – lacks rigor and precision and overlooks the fundamental building blocks of the reading experience. However, the three types of learning disability profile cited in Chapter 4 demonstrate that phonic principles are not equipped to fulfil that role either. These students need something still more fundamental, either as an alternative to phonic instruction, or as a precursor that enables them to access phonics more effectively.

That 'something else' is the visual recognition of the sequence of letters in a word. As explained in Chapter 4, recognition must precede decoding; the former can occur successfully without the latter, but the latter is entirely dependent on the former. A person with visual dyslexia who is seeing the word 'was' as 'saw' will not be able to decode the word, no matter how well he is instructed to do so.

Visual-sequential letter recognition is not whole-word recognition. It is a rigorous and precise analysis of components; a more precise starting point, in fact, than grapheme-phoneme correspondences. Letters are not sounds. They signal a certain sound in a certain context, but they have their own identity, as represented by their name. The letter *A* can produce six different sounds: ă as in *cat*, ā as in *ape*, **o:** as in *all*, **a:** as in *ask*, ĕ as in *any*, and ə as in *thinkable*. But the letter *A* is always called *A*.

In the past, some primary educators have recommended teaching children the most common sound that a letter makes *as if it were* its name. This was done with the best of intentions. In 2006, when volunteering as a dyslexia expert in a local primary school, I was told by a classroom aide to avoid using the names of letters as this would confuse the more severely dyslexic children in the class. I had to bite my tongue. In private practice, working one-to-one with older children who still struggle to read, I have seen the consequences of this approach first-hand: bewildered children who, when eventually taught the names of letters after spending several years identifying them by their sounds, hesitate when spelling out a word because each of the letters has a dual identity. Some children of later elementary or even middle school age had formed the impression that the letter names are the names of the upper-case letters and the sounds are the names of the lower-case letters. Not to mention the bizarre cartoonization of *c* as 'cuddly kə' and of *k* as 'kicking kə' ('Who is it kicking, Mommy?'...) to avoid the *complication* of using their actual names!

How did we ever come up with the idea that naming was a more advanced skill than decoding? Children assimilate names with explosive zest from the moment they start to learn language – after all, that is what learning language is. On arrival in school, they quickly and effortlessly learn the names of all the other thirty or so pupils in their class. The sounds made by each letter are their functions, not their identity. Once a child knows with certainty what *a* is called, the fact that it can make different sounds in different words is no more difficult a concept than the notion that Robert can be sitting, standing or hopping; that a dog can bark, growl or pant; that a door can be open or closed; and so on.

It is not as if, by teaching letter names first, we are giving children useless information they will never need. Mastery of the letter names is an essential life skill: they are darned useful when you need to instruct a hotel receptionist how to write your name, direct a visitor to 'Block C' at your workplace, or explain to someone how to spell *psyche*. Why protect young children from the easiest and most essential information about letters that they will ever need?

Davis Learning Strategies is a three-year reading teaching program that emphasizes the multisensory mastery of letters in a process based around their names. From a clear, simple template, children produce each letter through the explorative medium of white reusable modeling clay, visualize their creation, and name it. This process becomes the bedrock on top of which children master alphabetical order, discover the three parts of a word (appearance, sound, meaning), and take their first steps in word recognition. In a three-year pilot study involving three classes of differing socio-economic background, sight word recognition after the first year of intervention was significantly higher than that of the controls. What is more, at the end of the three-year pilot, no special education referrals had been made for any of the children in the three pilot classes (the children were by now aged 9).[39]

---

[39] (Pfeiffer, Davis, Kellogg, Hern, McLaughlin, & Curry, 2001)

What is particularly interesting about this approach is that it can be practiced either as an alternative to phonic instruction or together with it. Children can name the clay *A* they have created, saying simply, 'You are *A*;' or they can say to it, 'You are *A*; you say ă.' Phonic prodigies can even say: 'You are *A*; you say ă, ā, oː, aː, ĕ, or ə.' In this way, letter naming provides a universal starting point for literacy acquisition; it enables teachers to build a single, coherent structure for reading instruction that is founded on uniformly agreed principles, but that diversifies into different reading approaches depending on factors such as student age, background, and learning profile.

Here, for instance, is a possible skeletal outline for teaching reading to a child with good phonological awareness and no particular indicators of any learning disability:

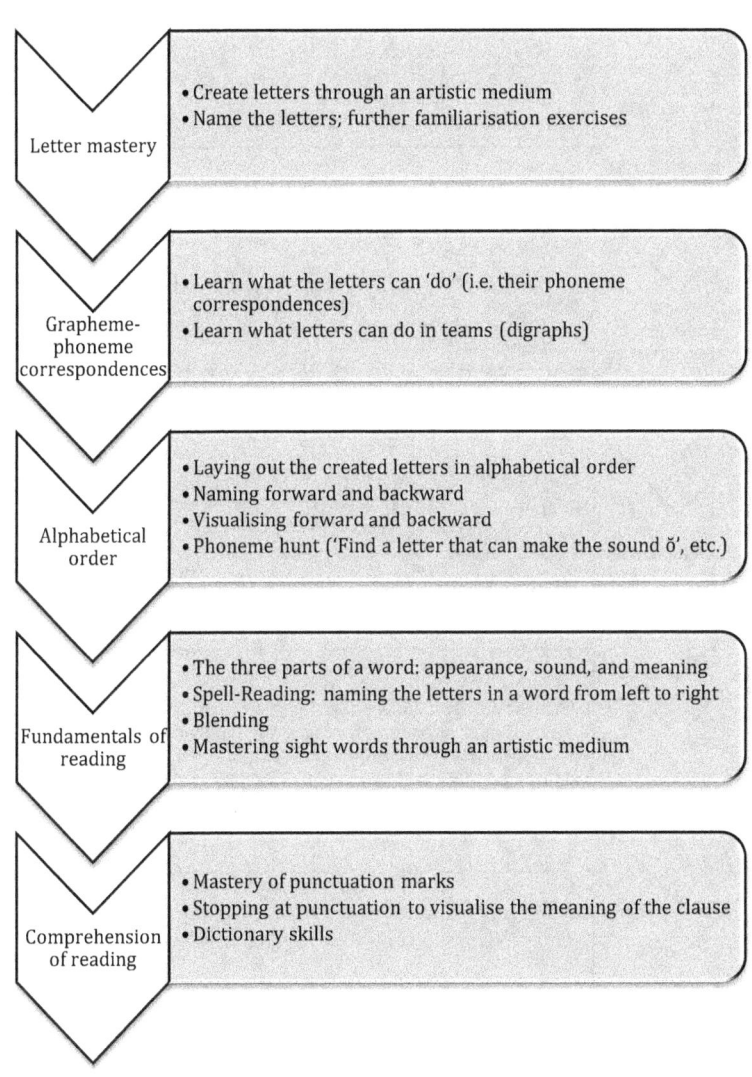

- **Letter mastery**
  - Create letters through an artistic medium
  - Name the letters; further familiarisation exercises

- **Grapheme-phoneme correspondences**
  - Learn what the letters can 'do' (i.e. their phoneme correspondences)
  - Learn what letters can do in teams (digraphs)

- **Alphabetical order**
  - Laying out the created letters in alphabetical order
  - Naming forward and backward
  - Visualising forward and backward
  - Phoneme hunt ('Find a letter that can make the sound ŏ', etc.)

- **Fundamentals of reading**
  - The three parts of a word: appearance, sound, and meaning
  - Spell-Reading: naming the letters in a word from left to right
  - Blending
  - Mastering sight words through an artistic medium

- **Comprehension of reading**
  - Mastery of punctuation marks
  - Stopping at punctuation to visualise the meaning of the clause
  - Dictionary skills

Here is a similar basic outline that could suit a child with poor phonological awareness, a non-native English profile, and/or visual stress:

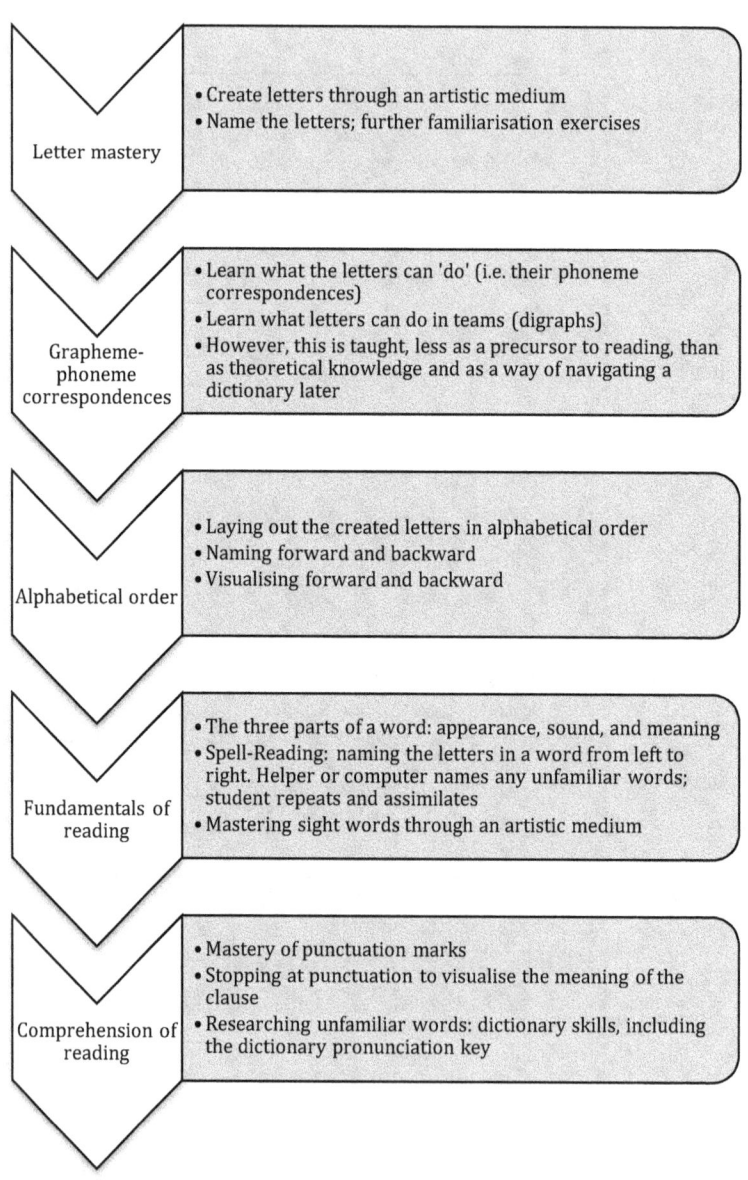

Letter mastery
- Create letters through an artistic medium
- Name the letters; further familiarisation exercises

Grapheme-phoneme correspondences
- Learn what the letters can 'do' (i.e. their phoneme correspondences)
- Learn what letters can do in teams (digraphs)
- However, this is taught, less as a precursor to reading, than as theoretical knowledge and as a way of navigating a dictionary later

Alphabetical order
- Laying out the created letters in alphabetical order
- Naming forward and backward
- Visualising forward and backward

Fundamentals of reading
- The three parts of a word: appearance, sound, and meaning
- Spell-Reading: naming the letters in a word from left to right. Helper or computer names any unfamiliar words; student repeats and assimilates
- Mastering sight words through an artistic medium

Comprehension of reading
- Mastery of punctuation marks
- Stopping at punctuation to visualise the meaning of the clause
- Researching unfamiliar words: dictionary skills, including the dictionary pronunciation key

The scope for differentiation should be obvious. By setting attainment targets based on fluency and accuracy of word recognition, educators are freed from ideological constraints as to how these targets are achieved, while remaining subject to success criteria that are arguably more rigorous than the old phonic ones were. The use of artistic media, such as modeling clay, gives all children a firm grounding in the identity of the letter symbols at the start of their literacy learning. Phonic methods remain center-stage in the classroom, as they are clearly the most effective route to reading for the majority of learners, but they are now reinforced by spell-reading techniques which anchor awareness of letter sequences so that decoding can be as effective as possible. The minority of children who will struggle with a phonic approach can be sent along a parallel track which keeps the same attainment targets but which continues to use a combination of spell-reading and dictionary skills for reading fluency and the acquisition of new reading vocabulary.

Spell-Reading has been central to the success that the Davis Learning Strategies have enjoyed. The procedure is explained in Chapter 11 of this book and is based on alert visual recognition of the sequence of letters in a word. While it is often assumed that phonic decoding is essential to the acquisition of new reading vocabulary, good dictionary skills can serve just as well. I have worked with many dyslexic learners who became remarkably quick at looking up words once they had a thorough visual-spatial mastery of alphabetical order.

Rudimentary familiarity with phonics is sufficient to enable a learner to take an educated guess as to what the first three letters of the word might be, and therefore, where to take their first stab in the dictionary. Many eBook-readers such as the Kindle provide a still faster route: clicking on an unfamiliar word takes one directly to a dictionary entry and definition. After all, phonic decoding does not tell a person what a word *means*; it cannot serve on its own as a means of increasing a person's vocabulary. What is more, with a little training, even dyslexic children with low phonological awareness seem to become adept at using the dictionary's pronunciation symbols to work out how an unfamiliar word is spoken.

The end-purpose of reading is to understand what has been read. If a fluent reader can move instantly and effortlessly between the printed word on the page and a mental image of what it means, does it matter whether that automated level of comprehension was acquired through a phonic or a non-phonic route? In fashioning a reading curriculum, we need to be mindful of the starting point A – the need to recognize the sequence of letters in a word – and the end goal B – fluent, accurate and comprehending reading. The route for getting from A to B can vary, and it should be plotted intelligently for each child.

Effortless, automated comprehension starts at word level, where the goal must be to build a fluent and accurate association between a word and what it means –

so when the reader sees the word *puppy*, for instance, a mental image of a young dog springs to mind unbidden. It is this automaticity that is thought to give rise to the so-called *Stroop effect*: in 1935, J. Ridley Stroop reported on a study in which he had asked seventy college undergraduates to engage with a sheet containing color names, each printed in a different color from the color that the word denoted.

BROWN	RED	BLUE	BLUE	RED
RED	PURPLE	GREEN	ORANGE	GREEN
ORANGE	BROWN	PURPLE	GREEN	PURPLE
GREEN	BLUE	ORANGE	BROWN	ORANGE
BLUE	ORANGE	RED	RED	BROWN
PURPLE	BROWN	BLUE	BLUE	GREEN
RED	PURPLE	BROWN	PURPLE	RED
GREEN	BLUE	BLUE	BROWN	PURPLE
BROWN	RED	RED	ORANGE	BLUE
ORANGE	BROWN	ORANGE	BLUE	GREEN
PURPLE	GREEN	PURPLE	BROWN	ORANGE
GREEN	ORANGE	GREEN	PURPLE	RED

Figure 10: a reconstruction of the Stroop Test (source and original color version: https://en.wikiversity.org/wiki/Psycholinguistics/Chronometry)

What emerged from the study was that, when participants were asked to name the color in which the word was written, they were much slower at doing so than when asked simply to read the words. From this, Stroop deduced that the recognition of familiar words in reading tends to have become more automated in adults even than the naming of colors.[40]

---

[40] (Stroop, 1935)

Now, one might think that the automaticity of the Stroop effect is a purely phonological process: that we link up graphemes and phonemes with such a high level of robotic fluency that it overrides our awareness of color. However, the *taboo Stroop effect*, as tested by Mackay et al in 2004 and cited by Steven Pinker in his book, *The Stuff of Thought*, suggests otherwise. In Mackay's test, participants were exposed, not to the names of colors printed in conflicting colors, but to a range of expletives such as *wh*re, f*ck, sh*t, c*ck* etc. (vowels are masked here for decorum, whereas Mackay's subjects were exposed to the full words in all their asterisk-free glory). As in the original Stroop test, subjects were asked to ignore the words and just name the colors in which they were written; this occurred across a series of taboo expletives as well as a series of neutral words. Compared to the neutral words, subjects named the colors of the taboo words significantly more slowly, and with a higher incidence of error.[41]

What this suggests is that the automaticity revealed in the Stroop testing is not just about associating a word with its sound, but that an instant association with meaning is involved. At the risk of stating the obvious, it is the meaning of taboo words that shocks the reader, not the way they sound. This meshes very well with the 'Dual Route' hypothesis of reading fluency that was discussed briefly in Chapter 1.

---

[41] (Mackay, et al., 2004)

As has likewise been seen in Chapter 1, automated comprehension tends to develop more easily for 'picture words' such as *tyrannosaurus, surprise, pink*, and *jump* than it does for abstract, high-frequency 'connectives' such as *if, the, because* and *unless*. These connectives probably make up the majority of words that we read, as well as giving expression to the kaleidoscope of connections that we learn to make between the things, qualities and events that life presents to us. Multisensory exploration of the meanings of these two hundred or so words can form an enriching element in an elementary school reading curriculum. Such exploration overcomes a key impediment to reading fluency for 'picture-thinking' dyslexic learners who stumble on the abstract, imageless nature of these words, while also serving as an important intellect-building exercise for all learners.

Davis Learning Strategies is a three-year reading teaching program delivered in primary and elementary school classrooms to children of all learning styles. A key element of the program is Davis Symbol Mastery, a multisensory word mastery process whereby pupils make their own creative depiction of the meanings of the high-frequency connectives, in clay. The letters of the word are then also made out of clay and the pupil speaks the word, thereby bringing all three parts of the word together in a single experience.

Figure 11: Davis Learning Strategies and basic sight words.

A three-year study of the effectiveness of Davis Learning Strategies, involving 86 primary school children in the San Francisco Bay Area, supports the hypothesis that multisensory mastery of high-frequency connectives enhances fluency of reading while also building intellect. After the first year of intervention, those first-grade children who had received Davis Learning Strategies instruction scored significantly higher than the control group for mastery of 100 basic sight words. (90-100% accuracy for all Davis classrooms vs. less than 67% accuracy for all control group classrooms).

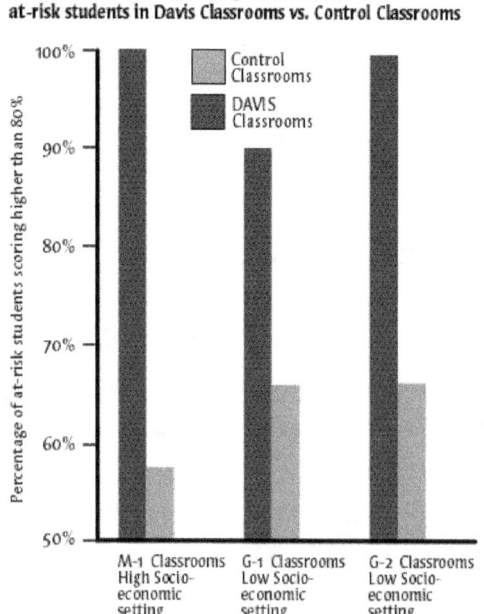

Figure 12: Davis Learning Strategies and basic sight words. Source: www.davislearn.com

Three years into the intervention, there had been no special education referrals from any of the Davis Learning Strategies classes, and – perhaps most significantly of all – Gifted and Talented (GATE) referrals were well above the federal average.[42] In the words of one student teacher, 'This is the gift that we are able to give our children if we implement the Davis Learning Strategies in our classrooms. We are able to give each learner, regardless of their individual learning style, the ability and opportunity to learn successfully. As educators, what greater reward do we require?'

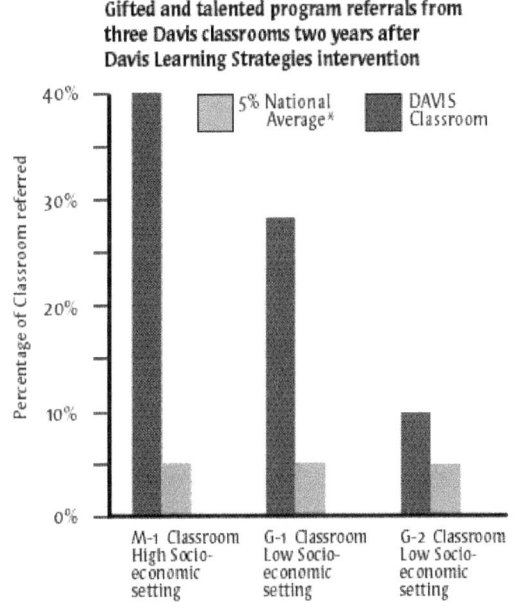

Figure 13: Davis Learning Strategies and GATE referrals. Source: www.davislearn.com

---

[42] (Pfeiffer, et al., 2001)

Further details of the Davis Symbol Mastery procedure are provided in Chapter 10 of this book.

Regardless of how fluency of word comprehension is developed, we need to engage our pupils' mental imagery, or 'picture thinking', more prominently. It would be good if there were more teacher-class dialogues along these lines: 'Can you picture what *tyrannosaurus* means?' 'Sure!' 'What about *if*? Can you picture what *if* means?' 'Em – no!' 'OK – let's explore *if* until we can picture it!'

We also need to exploit the power of mental imagery more fully in the processing of continuous text. Punctuation awareness is a key element here. Those punctuation marks that serve to separate one clause from the next – full stops, question marks, exclamation marks, dashes, semicolons, and commas – are signaling to the reader to stop and process meaning. The meaning of a completed clause can be either pictured or felt. 'The dog ran barking down the – ' does not form a satisfactory mental image. 'The dog ran barking down the street.' however, does. In the sentence, 'The dog ran barking down the street, its hackles raised and its teeth bared', the comma offers an appropriate place to break our mental image into two components if the length of the sentence would otherwise give us cognitive indigestion. For more on the power of combining punctuation with mental imagery to develop critical reading, see Chapter 11 of this book.

Chapter 6: ADHD and the Processing Speed Conundrum

'We all love H. Well, most of us that deal with him do. He has an incredible energy, bounce, intelligence and kindness; if he could bottle it, he would be a millionaire. Sadly, that career choice isn't available to him. What seems more likely, at the moment, is a career in Jackass, or Nitro Circus: his feats of daring-do – whether it is hopping from one end of the dorm to the other on his crutches, death-defying boarding past the Deputy Head[43] in the corridor or simply flying down the campus in a toy car – are always impressive.'

Thus began the concluding boarding housemaster's report of an endearingly hyperactive pupil at the end of Ninth Grade. I knew this pupil, and he was one of the quickest thinkers and quickest talkers one is likely to come across in secondary education. Not the sort of individual you would expect to be diagnosed with slow

---

[43] UK equivalent of Vice-Principal

visual-motor processing speed – yet this pupil qualified for a 25% additional time allowance in examinations for precisely that reason. Time and time again, I have seen pupils with attention focus and hyperactivity issues – kids well-known for running down corridors, tearing across sports fields, and talking the hind leg off a donkey – test as having low speed of processing.

In observing this, I am not alone. Jacobson et al studied 41 children with ADHD and found that they had reduced processing speed by comparison with the 21 controls.[44] The Joint Council for Qualifications has also latched onto this paradoxical correlation. Page 16 of its 2016-17 guidance to examination centers on Access Arrangements states, 'A diagnosis of ADD or ADHD should trigger the center to undertake a broad assessment of the candidate's speed of processing.' What is going on here?

Additude magazine offers to its ADD parent readership a functional but arid explanation: 'Slow processing speed means that he takes a bit longer than other kids his age to make sense of the information he takes in. He might have trouble assimilating written or spoken information, or take longer to answer questions or finish tests. This is not a matter of intelligence, as you know, but it does make it hard for him to demonstrate his knowledge.'[45]

And yet, another interpretation is possible that actually makes the ADHDer seem kinda cool. Essentially,

---

[44] (Jacobson, et al., 2011)
[45] (Additude, 2006)

processing speed tests examine our *linear* processing speed. Take the Symbol Digit Modalities Test (SDMT)[46], the visual-motor processing speed test by which the aforementioned pupil qualified for extra time in examinations. That test presents candidates with ten made-up symbols, each corresponding to a digit; candidates then have to fill in the correct digit under each symbol, working along each line from left to right. The number of correct answers completed in 90 seconds generates the candidate's score.

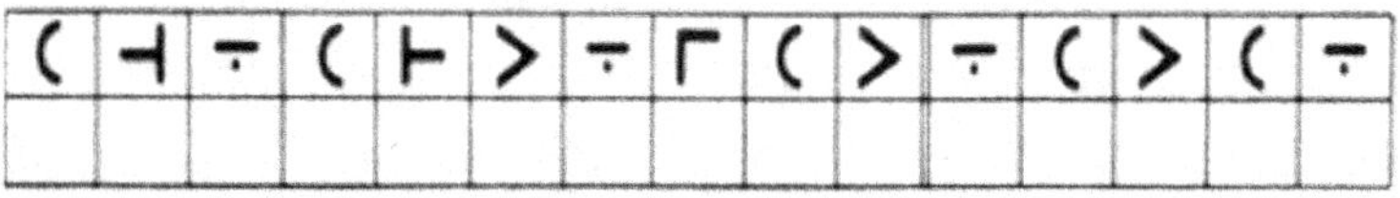

Figure 14: The top row of the Symbol Digit Modalities Test (Smith, 1982).

Now, ADHDers are renowned for the way in which they spread their attention over a wide field. 'Attention,' writes Sweitzer, '...is at the heart of the issue of ADHD, as the name Attention Deficit applies, and yet attention excess, as Dr Dodson calls it, is equally or even more of a problem in the disorder. The world is full of innumerable internal and external objects that, for better or worse, draw our attention... The ADHD brain loves multitasking because two or three things of even low-level interest are

---

[46] (Smith, 1982). Material from the SDMT copyright © 1973 by Western Psychological Services. Reprinted by R. Whitehead, Create-A-Word Books Ltd, for scholarly display purposes by permission of the publisher, WPS. Not to be reprinted in whole or in part for any additional purpose without the expressed, written permission of the publisher (rights@wpspublish.com). All rights reserved.

more stimulating than a single task of low-level interest.'[47]

A low score on a processing speed test does not have to mean the subject is a slow thinker. It can just as well mean that the subject, perhaps involuntarily, has had a hundred and one extraneous thoughts during the test. By their very design, processing speed tests tend to reward the more linear thinker and penalize the multitasker. They champion the pedestrian ambling along the public footpath and marginalize the guy on the Honda doing wheelies all over the parking lot.

'When my son, at age 13, was diagnosed with ADD and was told that he had a 'disease' that was 'similar to diabetes, but instead of your pancreas being damaged and not producing enough insulin, your brain has been damaged and isn't producing enough neurotransmitters,' I knew in my gut it was a lousy, disempowering story.'[48] Thus writes Thom Hartmann, author of a radical hypothesis that rejects traditional 'disability' theories of ADHD and instead sees ADHDers as hunters in a world of farmers. According to Hartmann, the traits of ADHD typically seen as deficits might well be construed as assets in a hunter civilization:

---

[47] (Sweitzer, 2014)
[48] (Hartmann, 2007)

Trait as it appears in the 'Disorder' view:	How it appears in the 'Hunter' view:	Opposite 'Farmer' traits:
Attention spans short, but can become intensely focused for the long periods of time.	Constantly monitoring their environment.	Not easily distracted from the task at hand.
Poor planner: disorganized and impulsive (makes snap decisions).	Able to throw themselves into the chase on a moment's notice.	Able to sustain a steady, dependable effort.
Distorted sense of time: unaware of how long it will take to do something.	Flexible; ready to change strategy quickly.	Organized, purposeful. They have a long-term strategy and they stick to it.
Impatient.	Tireless: capable of sustained drives, but only when 'Hot on the trail' of some goal.	Conscious of time and timing. They get things done in time, pace themselves, have good 'staying power.'
Doesn't convert words into concepts adeptly, and vice versa. May or may not have a reading disability.	Visual/Concrete thinker, clearly seeing a tangible goal even if there are no words for it.	Patient. Aware that good things take time – willing to wait.
Has difficulty following directions.	Independent.	Team player.

Trait as it appears in the 'Disorder' view:	How it appears in the 'Hunter' view:	Opposite 'Farmer' traits:
Daydreamer.	Bored by mundane tasks; enjoy new ideas, excitement, 'the hunt' being hot on the trail.	Focused. Good at follow-through, tending to details, 'taking care of business.'
Acts without considering consequences.	Willing and able to take risk and face danger.	Careful. 'looking before you leap.'
Lacking in the social graces.	'No time for niceties when there are decisions to be made!'	Nurturing; creates and supports community values; attuned to whether something will last.[49]

Is the cup half empty? Half full? Or rich in both water and atmospheric gases? In the final analysis, it matters little to an ADHDer whether we place a positive or negative spin on the way he thinks if we are unable to understand how his mind works and teach him accordingly.

Tests do not diagnose; people do. An astute assessor will not just cite a processing speed score, but will consider what that score *means* in the context of other testing and the broader knowledge of the subject that is

---

[49] (Hartmann, 2007)

available. A low processing speed score taken in isolation is of little use to a teacher. Taken together with high visual and/or verbal ability scores, and with holistic indicators of a sprightly attention, an *interpretation* of that score as a sign of a multi-tasking intelligence gives an educator something to chew on.

Chewing is one thing; swallowing quite another. Mental multi-tasking is an ability, not a disability. It is a way of thinking that has value. It should not be suppressed – through drugs, duress, or by any other means. Yet in some situations, the ability to think of just one thing at a time comes in very handy too. We need to be able to brainstorm ideas, to think outside the box – but then we need to select the best ideas and follow through on them, one step at a time. Sometimes, our mind needs to be a pullulating forest; at other times, Jack's beanstalk. Crucially, though, it needs to learn when to be which, and how to channel-hop from the one to the other with ease and instancy. How on earth does one teach that?

Lydia Zylowska's study into the feasibility of mindfulness meditation training as a treatment for ADHD provides a starting point. While the study was of a modest sample size of 23 adults and adolescents, pre- and post-testing using the Attention Network Test indicated a significant drop in attentional conflict (distractibility) in the majority of participants. Notably, the mean post-training ANT score of the test sample was comparable to mean scores found elsewhere in non-ADHD adult and adolescent samples.[50] In a separate study, twenty subjects with extensive experience in Insight meditation demonstrated 'thicker' (i.e. more developed) brain regions associated with attention, body awareness and sensory processing than did matched controls, including the prefrontal cortex and right anterior insula.[51]

Davis Orientation Counseling® is a simple, self-directed technique, devised by dyslexic author Ronald Davis, that trains children and adults to switch consciously between disorientation and orientation. Disorientation is a creative state in which the mind goes into itself in order to solve problems, daydream, or resolve confusion. Orientation is a receptive state in which the mind is present to the world around one: it sees what the eyes are seeing, hears what the ears are hearing, perceives stillness and movement accurately and experiences time consistently.

Davis Orientation Counseling is generally administered alongside a range of other Davis techniques designed to address literacy, numeracy and/or attention focus intervention. In 2005, René Engelbrecht of Stellenbosch University, South Africa, worked with a group of 20 Afrikaans-speaking pupils in grade 5-7 from a school for learners with special needs, to study the impact of a range of Davis techniques, including Davis Orientation Counselling. Alongside gains in reading and spelling ability, Engelbrecht reports significant gains in

---

[50] (Zylowska, et al., 2008)
[51] (Lazar, et al., 2005)

psychological measures such as attention focus, rule-observance, behavior, oppositional defiance, and several other emotional-behavioral categories.[52]

Similarly, researchers at University of the Free State in Bloemfontein, South Africa, monitored the progress of 18 students who were given instruction using Davis techniques (including Davis Orientation Counselling) over a period of nine months. Aside from progress in literacy, outcomes included the development of positive attitudes towards community engagement, students realizing their social responsibility, the gaining of insights into and understanding of social and educational issues, and finally the opportunity to develop lifelong learning and problem-solving skills.[53]

In 2003, a group of researchers in Italy evaluated the reading speed and accuracy of dyslexic students receiving eight different treatments, one of which was Davis Orientation Counselling, administered – unusually – in isolation from the other Davis techniques. The group receiving the Davis Orientation instruction comprised 16 students, grades 3-8. The Davis group showed the greatest increase in reading speed, with passage reading at a rate that was double or triple the speed of students in other groups.[54] Reading speed often correlates with stamina of attention focus.

---

[52] (Engelbrecht, 2005)
[53] (van Staden, et al., 2009)
[54] (Tressoldi, et al., 2003)

These modest but persistent indicators from small-group, qualitative studies suggest that issues of attention focus are *malleable* and will respond to the right kind of training. ADHDers do not need to suppress their multi-tasking, risk-taking talent; they just need to learn how to channel it. In his book, *Delivered from Distraction*, Edward Hallowell cites six lifestyle changes that can impact positively on ADHD: positive human contact, reducing exposure to electronic gadgets, improving sleep patterns, eating a balanced diet, regular exercise, and prayer or meditation. 'The goal,' states Hallowell, 'is to sculpt ADD into a blessing. You can do this by accentuating what's useful and paring back on what's not. Usually, that is not easy to do. For a few lucky people, it happens easily, but for most people such life-sculpting takes pains. Sometimes it seems futile. But I have seen too many people with ADD prevail over their problems ever to believe it's impossible. *Everyone* who has ADD can sculpt a fulfilling, joyful life out of what they've been born with.'[55]

In his book, *The Gift of Learning*,[56] Ronald Davis presents a detailed hypothesis as to the developmental effects of a mind prone to regular, protracted disorientation into an alternate reality that it has created – a kind of persistent deep-level daydream. 'The person's alternate reality experiences,' asserts Davis, 'have somehow excluded or missed important lessons that would prevent the unwanted behaviors of ADD.' Davis

---
[55] (Hallowell & Ratey, 2005)
[56] (Davis & Braun, 2003)

points out that an ADHDer's alternate reality is more than a common or garden reverie. 'They don't fit the model of an ordinary dream because the state of disorientation allows the dream to be experienced as reality... To others, [a child with ADD] is just playing by himself. To him it is his reality – his life. Even though he is just playing, the life lessons learned are incorporated into his filtering system.'

In this alternate reality, nothing exists permanently, so there is no past or present. When the ADHD child enters his own inner world, he is entering a perpetual alternate 'now'. Davis goes on to cite a whole host of concepts, ranging from *change, cause/effect, time, sequence* to *order vs. disorder* that can be replaced or altered as a result. Each of these can be thought of as life lessons that can consequently be missed or mis-learnt.

This chapter has already examined how techniques such as mindfulness and Davis Orientation Counseling have proven successful in showing ADHDers how to take control of the portal between this alternate world and the real, physical universe and decide which they wish to inhabit when. For ADHDers, the road to success and fulfilment is often a rocky one. Parents of an ADHDer often require nerves of steel: it is frightening to see your child engage in erratic, challenging and unpredictable behavior and to lead a life that doesn't seems to be 'going' anywhere. And yet ADHDers are full of surprises, and the biggest surprise of all may be what your ADHD child becomes as he emerges into adulthood. As a parent, your job is to believe in your child, to notice and comment on the good things he does, to avoid *evaluating* him as good or bad, and to ask any other adults in his life to do the same. In the words of the famous grandmother author duo Adele Faber and Elaine Mazlish: 'You can take away 'good boy' by calling him 'bad boy' the next day. But you can't ever take away from him the time he cheered his mother with a get-well card, or the time he stuck with his work and persevered even though he was very tired. These moments, when his best was affirmed, become lifelong touchstones to which a child can return in times of doubt or discouragement. In the past he did something he was proud of. He has it within him to do it again.'[57]

---

[57] (Faber & Mazlish, 2012)

How Homeschooling Set Me Free to Love My ADHD

(by my son, Philip Whitehead)

I was buying groceries the other day, when I noticed a boy in his school uniform arguing with his dad. Tired and frustrated, he held up his lunchbox and slammed it on the ground. A few parents looked on disapprovingly. I caught the boy's eye for a second and threw him a wink that said, 'Yeah, me too.' After all, that was me 15 years ago.

As a child, I was a parent's worst nightmare. I got on the wrong side of my teachers at nursery school, I shouted over everyone at dinner parties, and I even broke my parents' bed frame (they slept on the floor for a year thereafter).

Predictably, I didn't get on well when I started school. Being able to read placed me a step ahead of the other children, meaning that I wasn't allowed to answer any questions in class. That was fine by me. I found plenty of tables to draw on, paper balls to throw, and other kids whose ears I could flick from behind. Every day I was sent out of the classroom for misbehaving.

My parents realized that I probably wasn't being challenged enough by teachers droning on about things that didn't interest me. It was at this point that formal education and I decided to take a break from each other.

The silver lining was that my older brother also withdrew from school. The two of us spent time at home engaging in endless activities. We had a blast and learned a great deal, too. Invariably, my brother's maturity meant he could stick with things longer than I could. He patiently sat and learned new skills, like perspective drawing or dancing. I tested the durability of chess figurines in a self-devised chess-piece-versus-table-top competition.

It soon became clear that I was 'different.' There was the time I broke a playmate's leg during some overzealous play fighting; the afternoon I hit my brother over the head with a hammer playing 'police vs. burglars'; and the unforgettable day my violin teacher refused to teach me anymore on the grounds that I was uncontrollable. So what was the solution—send me to my room? I would just empty all the bookshelves and bang on the walls. No, there had to be another way.

Eventually, Mom and Dad reached their wits' end. Left with no other option, they stopped trying. I don't mean they gave up on me. Loving parents don't neglect their own child, no matter how irksome he is. Neglect and creative freedom, however, are different.

My parents, acting as teachers, stepped back and let me write my own syllabus. Of course, the syllabus changed daily: on Mondays, I read astronomy books and talked nonstop about quasars; on Tuesday mornings, I wrote poems or made clay pottery. The important thing was not what I was learning, but that I was learning. By allowing me to learn whatever I chose, my parents enabled me to motivate myself. This led me down lots of intellectual paths and allowed me to assimilate volumes of knowledge about certain subjects, just as anyone can when they are passionate about something.

Sure, I wasted time climbing trees while other kids were working hard at school, but I never wasted a second trying to learn something I had no interest in. When I did eventually go back to school, there were some pretty hefty knowledge gaps to fill in, but my mental faculty was so well practiced that it took hardly any time at all for me to catch up.

Nowadays, I have learned to harness the upside of my short attention span. I run around daily forgetting what it was that I was so keen on accomplishing the day before, and I never cease to find new pointless avenues to focus all of my attention on — for no other reason than the sheer joy of learning. I have planners and apps to help me keep track of things, so I have no intention of 'squashing' my hyperactivity. It's what helped me attain a first-class honors degree, and it has always been the greatest tool in my arsenal of employable skills. My racing mind enables me to solve problems efficiently and to multitask with ease.

Maybe I regret winking at the kid in the supermarket. Maybe I should have gone up to his dad and said, 'It's OK. He's just not made to fit into that uniform. Not quite yet, anyhow.'[58]

---

[58] (Whitehead, 2016)

Chapter 7: Working Memory, or Feeling Memory?

A number of years ago I conducted a telephone consultation with a lady in her forties. This lady had a diagnosis of dyslexia, and had contacted me because she wanted to explore why she had found literacy-based tasks difficult at school, and continued to do so into adulthood.

In my experience, it is impossible to give a person meaningful insight into the nature of their learning disability until you also know their learning strengths. So I asked this lady what she was good at.

'Well,' she replied, 'I've always been good at math, right from an early age. And I've always been good at memorizing telephone numbers.'

'That's interesting,' I remarked. 'Do you know how you recall a telephone number when you need it?'

'Well,' the lady responded, 'I'm a very visual thinker. When I use my imagination, I think in pictures. So when I need to recall a telephone number, I just see it in front of me, as if it were on a screen.'

We then proceeded to explore what this lady found challenging. 'I'm a poor speller, and always have been,' she said.

Then a thought occurred to us both at the same time. What was enabling this lady to see a series of numerals clearly in her mind, but not a series of letters?

The more one reflects on this question, the more it challenges some of the assumptions that exist around the origins of dyslexia and other learning disabilities. The research and hypotheses around what causes dyslexia are complex, variegated, and not easy to summarize. Specific neurological deficits have been posited that include:

- Geschwind and Galaburda's *theory of cerebral lateralization*: simply summarized, that heightened levels of fetal testosterone slow development of the left hemisphere and account for a range of learning difficulties including stuttering, dyslexia and autism[59];
- Stein's *magnocellular deficit theory*, which asserts that impairment in the development of magnocells – a set of neurons responsible for perceiving location and movement – impairs the visual recognition of words in dyslexia[60];

---

[59] (Geschwind & Galaburda, 1987)
[60] (Stein, 2001)

- Nicolson and Fawcett's *cerebellar deficit hypothesis*, which suggests that impairments to the cerebellum or 'hind-brain' may hinder the development of automaticity across a range of skills affecting reading and writing[61];
- Shaywitz et al's observations of a *disruption of left-hemisphere posterior neural systems* in child and adult dyslexic readers when they perform reading tasks[62].

Others, such as Ute Frith, have suggested a multi-layered combination of biological, cognitive and behavioral causes of dyslexia[63]. A number of researchers and writers, and notably Maggie Snowling[64], support a phonological deficit hypothesis: that difficulties with the recognition and/or categorization of different speech sounds underlie dyslexic difficulties. Gradually, it seems that investigations are shifting from purely 'poking around the brain' into the more enigmatic realm of the relationship between mind and brain – between the grey matter vehicle and how it is driven.

And yet, the case of my telephone-number-savant-but-poor-speller lady consultee demands a still more sophisticated approach. Both letter sequences (e.g. words) and numeral sequences (e.g. telephone numbers) can be visualized. Visual thinkers who are good spellers will often tell you that they can 'see' words in their mind,

---

[61] (Fawcett & Nicolson, 2004)
[62] (Shaywitz, et al., 2006)
[63] (Frith & Frith, 1998)
[64] (Snowling, 2000)

similarly to how this lady could 'see' telephone numbers. So what are we to make of someone who, like this lady, can visualize one set of symbols but not another? A deficit-based model for dyslexia assumes that the difficulties stem from something in the brain and/or mind that is not functioning as it should – but can there really be an impairment that stops a person from visualizing *f-r-i-e-n-d* but allows them to visualize *2-6-5-4-9*?

When we pursue this line of enquiry, we find more anomalies. For instance, I have encountered dyslexic graphic designers who can clearly visualize the layout of a web design project, in all its complexities, but cannot use that same skill in order to visualize accurately the layout of a five-letter word. I have spoken to a dyslexic carpenter and fitter who told me that he never needed an instruction manual because he could always picture in his mind how the kitchen he was building would fit together. But again, he couldn't picture how a word would fit together.

When you engage with dyslexic thinkers in conversations of this kind, you find that dyslexia is rarely about a missing skill; far more often, it is about a skill that may be well-developed in some areas of life, but that cannot be used in certain others. This seems like a bizarre set of anomalies – it is like finding a person who has learnt to walk, and can do so on carpets and floorboards, but not on tiles.

If this is the case, then we need to look more intelligently at the stimulus – the word, number, or other set of symbols – that the learner is trying to assimilate. We need to look at how one kind of stimulus may affect a learner differently from another: in the case of my telephone contact, for instance, how letter symbols affected her differently from numerals. What this means, essentially, is that we need to look at emotion.

Joseph LeDoux was the first researcher to discover that the amygdala – a brain structure linked to fear responses and to pleasure – registers external stimuli much faster than does the 'rational' neocortex.[65] In his book, *Emotional Intelligence*[66], Daniel Goleman used the research of LeDoux and others to explain how, when the amygdala processes a stimulus as a threat, it 'hijacks' every other part of the brain, including the neocortex, to its fight-or-flight agenda. Thereby, the neocortex loses some of its ability to make subtle distinctions and becomes more 'binary' in the way it processes.

This comparatively recent discovery that we feel before we think, driven by innovations in neuroimaging, has spawned a whole array of advances in the human sciences. In psychotherapy, it has caused Joe Griffin and Ivan Tyrrell of the UK-based Human Givens Institute to challenge Albert Ellis' 'ABC' theory – a theory that lies at the heart of cognitive behavioral therapy (CBT) – that our behaviors are dictated by our beliefs[67]. Instead, Griffin and Tyrrell propose an 'APET' model, hypothesizing that

---

[65] (LeDoux, 2002)
[66] (Goleman, 1996)
[67] (Ellis, 1957)

an external stimulus (A = activating agent) is quickly categorized (P = pattern-matched), then processed by the amygdala (E = emotion) and only then by the conscious brain (T = thought).[68] The new 'we-feel-before-we-think' paradigm is also implicit in the principles underpinning the innovative discipline of behavioral economics: in his book, *Predictably Irrational*, behavioral economist Dan Ariely challenges the more traditional economist's perspective that rational behaviors underpin our economic decisions. Using Dr Jekyll and Mr Hyde as a metaphor, Ariely claims that each of us is an 'agglomeration of multiple selves', and that we will take different decisions depending on our level of emotional arousal.[69]

By contrast, LeDoux's and Goleman's work on the relationship between emotion and thought has hardly influenced thinking in educational psychology or the study of learning differences at all. It is high time that it did. On the surface, it may seem there is little in the letter z, the plus sign, or the formula for a quadratic equation that could arouse emotion. Yet learning is the assimilation of meaning, and the absence of meaning evokes the feeling of confusion. And understanding how confusion affects cognition unlocks a whole new way to understand learning difficulties and how they can be addressed.

---

[68] (Griffin & Tyrrell, 2001)
[69] (Ariely, 2008)

In learning, meaning could be defined as seeing how something newly encountered relates to one's existing experiences. When this occurs, the new piece of knowledge becomes absorbed into the matrix of existing experiences. This is another way of saying that it is assimilated into the learner's identity, which in turn is a way of saying that the person's identity grows.

When knowledge or ideas are presented to us that have no link in to our existing experience matrix, the result is confusion. Confusion is the feeling we have when confronted with something of unknown identity or function. This is another way of saying that we cannot place that 'something' anywhere within the existing framework of our knowledge and experience.

But more importantly, confusion is a highly unpleasant mental experience that is akin to our sense of danger. Consider how threatening it is to hear a sound or see movement in the bushes without being able to identify its source. When the feeling of confusion is experienced in sufficient measure, it is highly plausible that our amygdala could be aroused; this, in turn, would influence all of our cognitive functions.

All of this is a fancy-schmancy way of saying that some learning stimuli can be assimilated and stored easily, whereas others scramble our mental clarity. For the lady whose case we discussed at the beginning of this chapter, letters evoked confusion and thence cognitive distortion, while numerals did not. She could not spell, but she could recite telephone numbers. Dyslexics, when reading and writing, experience confusion. All along, the world had assumed that dyslexia was the cause, and confusion the effect. From what we now know about the amygdala and their effect on our cognitive functioning, it appears that it could the other way around: the emotion of confusion may itself be causing and embedding the symptoms of dyslexia.

Davis has fashioned a simple model for the way in which confusion may cascade down into the mistakes and distortions that we recognize as dyslexia. As was seen in the previous chapter, Davis coins the term *disorientation* to refer to a mental state in which the mind turns in on itself and creates its own alternate reality. Disorientation is a natural reaction to the state of confusion: when the mind feels threatened by an unrecognized stimulus in the environment, it can use disorientation as a problem-solving crucible, sifting through all sorts of possible answers to 'What could this be?' until it finds one that seems satisfactory.

Crucially, though, while disoriented, we experience our imagination as if it were reality. When we sit in a stationary train and watch an adjacent train move off, we feel as if we are – really and truly – moving. For a split-second, our eyes tell us we are moving, while our body tells us we are not. Disorientation synthesizes the feeling of movement to resolve this impossible contradiction. We are mistaken, but blissfully so: disorientation has provided an answer, and although it is a wrong answer, making a mistake is better than the paralyzing confusion that occurs when we have no answer at all.[70]

Recently, I have been working with a fourteen-year-old girl whom we shall call Emma. Emma is a pupil at an institution where I am employed to deliver one-to-one special education lessons. Emma is ambidextrous and can write equally fluently with either hand. When we started working together, the concepts *left* and *right* had no meaning for her, as there was effectively no difference between her experience of one side of her body and the other. Over a protracted period, I helped her build an awareness of these two concepts: through Davis-based focus and balance techniques, through body awareness exercises, through throwing and catching exercises in which Emma would name the hand with which she was catching the ball, and through a clay modeling process based on the principles of Davis Symbol Mastery and on a technique devised by Ioannis Tzivanakis.[71]

Emma is now so fluent in her naming of *left* and *right* that it no longer requires any reinforcement in our twice-weekly sessions. She is well-oriented in physical space and is an able sportswoman. However, when it comes to the world of symbols – letters, numerals, words – she has been prone to prolific reversals which have required a great deal of work to resolve. 3 could be written as 'Ɛ', 13

---

[70] (Davis, 1985)
[71] (Tzivanakis, 2003)

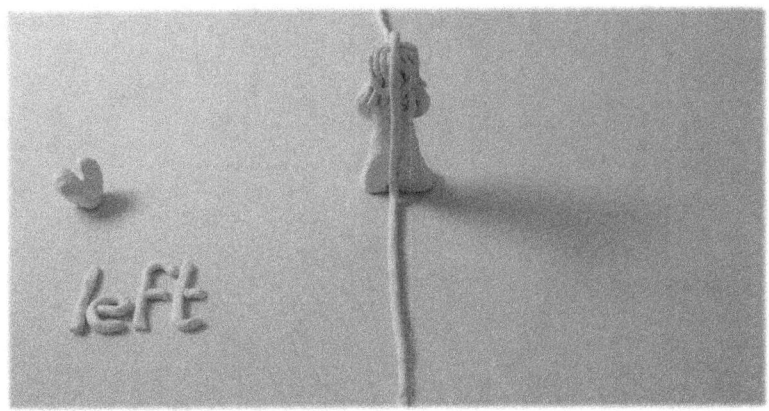

Figure 15: The Davis-Tzivanakis technique for mastery of the concept of 'left'. The clay model, made by the student, depicts the student herself and is positioned facing away from her so that the left side of the model is aligned with the left side of the student

as 'Ɛ1', *diamond* as 'mybunb' in a combination of spelling errors, displacements and reversals, and so on.

Recently, Emma was working in our sessions on the stability of her mental images of a number of lower-case letters that were causing her confusion. We were using a creative adaptation of the Davis Alphabet Mastery technique: Emma had made the entire alphabet out of clay and was exploring which of the letters she could visualize clearly when she closed her eyes. On some letters, she reported a vivid form of disorientation reaction: 'It's just like the feeling I get when I am walking down the stairs carrying a basket of washing and I miss a step'.

All of the letters that provoked this reaction were asymmetrical letters such as *q, p, k, j, g*. These were letters

Figure 16: The Davis Alphabet Mastery technique

on which Emma was prone to prolific reversals. Emma resolved her confused relationship with each letter by closing her eyes, visualizing the letter, opening her eyes, 'projecting' the visualized letter onto a sheet of A4 paper, then writing over her mental image in marker pen, producing several big versions of the letter in this way until the process of writing it felt certain and automatic.

This process worked well until we reached letter *e*. On this letter, Emma turned the letter over, looked it in reverse, and then said – somewhat indignantly: 'Why can't it be *e* when it is that way around?' Her thoughts turned to her mobile 'phone. 'My 'phone is my 'phone whether I am looking at it from the front or from the back; so why can't it be the same with a letter?' Gradually, she became reconciled to the idea that a letter's identity is formed not just from the symbol itself, but also from the direction from which we are looking at it. As we were discussing it, however, I could understand how outlandish this notion could seem. Imagine having a friend whom you had to call 'John' whenever you were looking at the right-hand side of his face and 'Fred' whenever you were looking at the left-hand side. This is essentially what we are expecting children to do when we tell them to differentiate *b* from *d* and *p* from *q*. No wonder that some of the more explorative and willful minds rebel.

> A number of years ago, I worked with a fifteen-year-old boy who had handwriting difficulties and whom we shall call Luke. As a first step, I asked Luke to make the alphabet out of clay and took him through the Davis Alphabet Mastery procedure. As part of the procedure, he looked in turn at each letter, touched the letter, and named it, using the Davis Orientation technique to monitor his mental state as he did so.
>
> When he reached the letter *i*, he reported an odd feeling of breathlessness. I asked him when he had had that feeling in his life before. He thought for a moment and then said, 'Once, when I was six, I was lying on my bunk bed, flicking through a picture book. Suddenly, I lost my balance and fell off. It was the top bunk, and I winded myself when I hit the floor.' He then told me that his handwriting difficulties centered around producing the vertical lines contained in letters such as *i, j, k, l* etc. He said that, when writing letter *i*, he would write it as a mere kink, giving it virtually no height at all.

> Outlandish as the association might seem, we went with it. Once the source of the feeling had been thus identified, Luke was able to separate his experience of the letters from the bunk-bed accident. By the end of the day, following a brief session of handwriting tuition, Luke was writing in a flowing, confident style that surprised not only him, but also his mother when she collected him at the end of the day.

When subtle perplexities of these kinds embed themselves into the basic symbols of our written language, the feeling of confusion will be relayed onwards into any more complex constructions that utilize those symbols. If you are confused about the identity of the letters *b* and *d*, how can you ever feel complete certainty when reading the words *bed*, *debt*, *bread*, *dread*, and so on? The frisson of confusion, even if imperceptibly subtle, will affect all processes of cognition and retention relating to the words in question.

The impact of confusion on cognition and retention becomes palpable when we scratch the surface of the working memory concept. Working memory is a useful theoretical construct, devised originally in the 1970s by Alan Baddeley and Graham Hitch [72] as a way of understanding how multiple pieces of data are stored in short-term memory and manipulated mentally – for example, when performing mental arithmetic or solving a riddle. It is commonly assumed that a given individual has

---

[72] (Baddeley & Hitch, 1974)

a fixed working memory capacity that does not vary fundamentally from task to task.

Yet there is growing evidence that working memory is reactive and fluctuating, not a rigid vessel with a fixed cognitive capacity. In 2007, Ashcraft and Krause found that individuals who experienced performance anxiety in mathematics demonstrated working memory restrictions when asked to do two-column addition in combination with a letter recall task.[73] They conclude that high math anxiety functions like an additional task, consuming working memory resources and leaving the individual with reduced capacity for the actual task being performed.

If working memory is vulnerable to anxiety, it stands to reason that it should be vulnerable to confusion too. Should this be the case, then one would expect working memory capacity to vary, perhaps wildly, depending on the nature of the things one is trying to put into it. In my experience, this is exactly what happens. As a diagnostician, I have often observed significant fluctuations between a person's performance across different subtests of the same working memory test battery. To gain more of a bird's eye view of this curious phenomenon, I recently collated the results of the twenty-one teenage subjects whose working memory I have tested over the past two years using five sub-tests of the Reynolds and Bigler Test of Memory and Learning

---

[73] (Ashcraft & Jeremy, 2007)

(Second Edition)[74]. The sub-tests used were: Digit Recall Forward; Letter Recall Forward; Manual Imitation; Digit Recall Backward; and Letter Recall Backward. The collation is shown below:

Subject	Digits Forward	Letters Forward	Manual Imitation	Digits Backward	Letters Backward
A. B.	10	10	13	10	14
A. Y.	5	12	12	13	14
A. T.	10	9	14	11	10
C. E.	5	9	7	14	12
D. R.	11	11	12	12	12
E. B.	11	7	13	10	7
E. G.	12	7	13	10	14
E. K.	4	8	8	9	8
E. M.	8	6	11	9	8
J. C.	8	7	11	13	10
J. D.	7	9	9	8	8
J. F.	7	5	6	8	8
L. C.	5	8	12	9	11
L. M.	9	9	9	9	8
M. H.	10	7	12	6	9
N. G.	6	8	12	9	10
R. C.	6	9	14	7	8
V. K.	6	6	6	7	7
V. V.	7	5	11	9	6
W. G.	14	12	12	8	8
W. L.	10	11	9	9	11

---

[74] (Reynolds & Bigler, 2007)

The scores are cited as so-called scaled scores – an age-related standardization system where 10 is the mean, 7 is the lower boundary of the average range, and 13 is the upper boundary thereof. Shade-coding the different ranges of scores tells a striking story. A. Y. and C. E. are atrocious at recalling digits forward but emerge as prodigies when doing the same thing with letters. E. B. shows a similar pattern, but in reverse. R. C. grapples in vain with mathematical digits, yet when repeating hand gestures in the Manual Imitation subtest he proves quite the whizz with his anatomical ones. Only D. R., L. M. and V. K. remain stoically monochrome across all five subtests.

More investigation is needed into the effect on our cognition of our *relationship* with what we are learning. We need to abandon the 'tough it out' school of education and encourage our students to become more self-aware. We need to develop frameworks that allow our children to explore their feelings and reactions as they encounter new learning facts – especially in the early years. Mindful approaches to education can provide early detection systems for the feeling of confusion, while multisensory techniques involving the pupil's own creativity can replace it with the feeling of certainty and ownership.

Davis Alphabet Mastery exemplifies how this can be done. At the end of the process, a proud dyslexic child (or adult) is able to recite the alphabet both forward and backward with their eyes closed – not in a rote-learnt, parrot fashion, but from a stable mental image of each letter, one after another, in sequence. Whether this procedure is enhancing working memory, or bypassing its restrictions by accessing long-term experiential memory, is a matter for neuropsychologists. What it does show is that, given the right internal and external environment, a proper process, and a proper *relationship* with each stimulus encountered, even students with diagnosed working memory restrictions can hold a great deal of information in their awareness and can reproduce it accurately.

Part Two of this book deals with a whole range of techniques that provide for permanent, sustainable learning.

Part II – The Tyrannosaurus Unleashed

Chapter 8: The Davis Learning Strategies

The Davis methods were conceived by Ronald Dell Davis after a personal breakthrough in overcoming his own severe dyslexia in 1980, when Davis was 38 years old. After a period of independent research and collaboration with experts in many fields, Ron Davis and Dr Fatima Ali opened the Reading Research Council in 1982 in Burlingame, California, which provided individualized dyslexia correction programs to children and adults.

In 1994, Davis published the first edition of his book, *The Gift of Dyslexia – Why Some of the Brightest People Can't Read... and How They Can Learn.* The book was rapidly translated into several other languages, and Davis Dyslexia Association International was established to provide professional training in the Davis methods across the world. There are now several hundred Davis Facilitators offering services in more than 30 languages and more than 40 countries worldwide.

The Davis Dyslexia Program was developed as a one-to-one, intensive program for children aged 8 and above, and for adults. The basic ideas underlying the Davis Dyslexia Program have been expanded into separate, tailored programs for Attention Mastery, Math Mastery, and Autism.

In the early 1990s, Ron Davis was approached by Sharon Pfeiffer, a primary school teacher in the San Francisco Bay Area, for advice on how to enhance the learning of pupils in her class who were struggling to make progress. The success that Pfeiffer experienced when implementing that advice led her to join Ron Davis and Fatima Ali at the Reading Research Council. As she immersed herself further in the Davis approach to learning, she maintained her existing links with her own school and with other schools in the same area, training other teaching colleagues in the basic approach. Ultimately, this led to the development of Davis Learning Strategies, a whole-class approach to reading teaching that revolves around the essential learning principles espoused in the first half of this book. A three-year pilot study of the strategies demonstrated an exciting impact both on the prevention of learning disabilities and on the levels of able and talented pupils in the pilot classes, as cited in detail in Chapter 5 of this book.

> In 1994, my son's life was turned around when we tried a few simple exercises that we found in a newly released book, *The Gift of Dyslexia*, by Ron Davis. After years of struggle, tears, frustration and anger, my son's

> reading problems seemed to dissipate almost magically, within less than an hour after we began the first exercise described in the book. The pain of reading gave way to a joyful rush of discovery, with my son eager to practice new-found skills. The little boy, then 11, who had struggled with 3rd grade material became a voracious reader, exceeding grade level within a few months of practice.
>
> I was delighted and amazed at the rapid changes I saw in my son, but I was soon disappointed to learn that many educators were skeptical of his approach. Despite the fact that Ron Davis had a 15-year proven track record before writing the first edition of his book, his work was rebuffed by many educators and established dyslexia organizations because of his innovative and novel approach.
>
> Abigail Marshall,
> Webmaster and Information Services Director,
> Davis Dyslexia Association International

The Davis approach relies on using the mental talents that dyslexic people and many other struggling learners share to overcome their learning problems. Rather than drill or repetition, the approach places emphasis on the quality of a single, meaningful learning experience – known in the Davis approach as *mastery*. Key ingredients of mastery are:

- a state of relaxed alertness. The learner's mind needs to be in a state where perceptions are accurate, and it needs to be free from stress. In the Davis approach, learners are given conscious control of their acuity through a set of mental techniques that have some commonality with mindfulness;

- active, experiential learning. To own a learning experience, the learner needs to invest in its creation. This is achieved through a combination of active visualization and the use of multisensory media, notably reusable modeling clay;

- a semiotic approach to learning which brings the signifier and the signified together in a single experience. In lay terms, this means that words, numerals, and other symbols such as mathematical signs are mastered together with their meaning.

Dear Richard,

I thought it only fair to share some information about Eden Trainor whom you worked with several years ago. Eden came to your base with Lynn his mother and spent a week working with you and your colleagues to help him develop strategies both to understand and to deal with the issues raised by his dyslexia.

Eden was generally disengaged from school work and performing poorly. However, within a year of working with you, he rapidly rose to the 'top sets' in virtually every subject – including English – and got a reasonable set of GCSE results[75]. Moving to the sixth form, it was clear to us that Eden could focus on those subjects he loved and was really good at and with a wee bit of encouragement could do really well.

He has recently been awarded the chance to study Physics at St Catherine's College, Oxford and is doing really well in his Maths, Further Maths, and Physics A Levels. We hope, and indeed expect, that he will get the grades that he needs to take up his place at Oxford.

Upon reflection, my wife and I, and Eden acknowledge the significant turning point in his life that was facilitated by your help. We cannot thank you enough, and wish that you would share in the joy and excitement of Eden doing so well, and the pivotal role that you were able to play in making his life opportunities better.

Thanks to you and your team.'

– Nick Trainor

[Eden received a Davis Dyslexia Program from me in 2007]

While the Davis methods revolve around standardized programs with a fixed set of key ingredients, they also

---

[75] GCSEs are UK school qualifications typically taken at the age of 16. They are similar in structure to the high school diploma, though tailored to a younger age.

provide for an open system of teaching and learning that can be used by educators in a number of different settings. The core principles outlined above, together with a working knowledge of some key techniques, can furnish a teacher 'toolkit' which can support potentially struggling learners while also enhancing the learning of the academically adept.

The following chapters of this book will outline some key Davis techniques and their possible applications, provide pointers for finding out more, and offer some sample teaching modules that demonstrate creative applications of Davis core principles. The modules have been developed in a one-to-one special education context but lend themselves to adaptation to whole-class settings.

> In 2013, I trained in the Davis Learning Strategies. I was very impressed by the DLS tools that were so simple to use yet had an amazing impact on all learners. In 2014, I completed my training as a Davis Facilitator. During that year, the school I work for had a total student strength of 4,500. I was aware that at least 10% students were struggling to learn in all the class rooms. It was impossible for me to reach out to all the students scattered around in so many different class rooms. With the support of the school management and especially the Chairman, Mr P. R. Krishna, we started the 'Indigo Section' for all the learners from grade I to VII who struggled to keep pace with the school curriculum. Indigo Sections became the model class rooms where DLS were

used for imparting all the concepts.

Now, as we step into the third year of our rendezvous with DLS, we have amazing experiences to share. The first batch of 11 students, who received instructions through DLS when they were in Grade-VII, have completed their Grade-X exams. Out of 11 students, 10 students scored more than 70% in their secondary school board exams.

The student performance record of last three years shows that all the children in Indigo section improve their reading skills by at least one to two levels every year. Their attention span increases, and they are able to understand the concepts better. Their critical thinking and reasoning skills improve. They enter the Indigo Section with low self-esteem and a lot of behavioral issues. But they leave Indigo section for the mainstream class rooms with amazing confidence, self-regulated responsible behavior, and ability for independent learning.

The mental self-regulation tools Release, Focus and Energy Dial have not just helped the students but also the teachers. The teachers are able to let out stress by using Release and feel motivated to use Focus and the Energy Dial to enhance their own potential. Many children have introduced the DLS tools to their parents.

LMOIS now has 115 DLS-trained teachers, three DLS Mentors and two licensed Davis Facilitators.

I strongly believe that the Davis Learning Strategies bring about holistic growth in a child. They not only help him excel in learning, but they also develop his overall personality and make him an independent learner.

I will always remain grateful to Ron Davis for giving the world this remarkable tool.

With warm regards,

Priti Venkatesan

HoD Special Education, Davis Facilitator and DLS Mentor, Lalaji Memorial Omega International School (LMOIS), Chennai, India

Chapter 9: Priming the Mind – Davis Focusing Strategies

As educators, we may have found ourselves in situations where we had to ask a learner to 'pay attention'. But what if the learner responded by asking, 'How?' Most conventional teacher training does not equip us to answer that question. Davis Focusing Strategies, however, do.

The strategies address three distinct aspects of focusing:

- the Release procedure shows learners how to eliminate physical and mental stress, including negative emotions which could impair the learning process;

- the Focus procedure trains learners to switch consciously between a creative, problem-solving mode of thinking where the mind turns in on itself – known in the Davis methods as *disorientation* – and an alert, receptive mode in which perception of one's environment is accurate – known in the Davis methods as *orientation*. Orientation is further enhanced through the use of exercises involving physical balance and hand-to-eye coordination;

- the Dial procedure trains learners to adjust their personal energy to a level optimum for the task in hand. Generally speaking, for instance, physical education will require higher levels of energy than most academic activities, whereas artistic endeavors will require a wide range of energy levels depending on whether the emphasis is on vigor or on fine detail control.

This chapter provides instruction in the Davis Release procedure. I have used this procedure with learners successfully in isolation as a strategy to combat performance anxiety, emotional agitation, and fatigue. What follows now is a brief, simplified version of the procedure that may be appropriate for use with whole classes in a primary school context. Teachers wishing to access a more in-depth version of the Release procedure, suitable for one-on-one instruction, can do so by purchasing a copy of *The Gift of Dyslexia* by Ronald Davis and/or by attending training workshops provided by their regional Davis Association. *The Gift of Dyslexia* also includes instruction in one-on-one Focus procedures known as Orientation Counseling and Alignment, and in the Dial procedure.

The Davis Release Procedure
(for classroom use)

Preparation:

As a class, discuss what a sigh means. Explain that it must be an audible sound such as 'ahhhh'. Without the sound, it is just a breath.

Procedure:

Have the students sit comfortably in their chairs and close their eyes.

Tell the students:

Sit comfortably in your chair.

Close your eyes.

Breathe in... hold it for a second or two.... let the air rush out of your mouth with an 'ahhhh' sound.

Do another sigh and feel the sigh all the way out to the tips of your fingers and toes.

Do another sigh and get that feeling all through your body.

Keep that feeling in your body.

That feeling is called Release.

Open your eyes.

Think Release and get that feeling.

Copyright © 1999, 2004 by Davis Dyslexia Association International. All rights reserved. Reproduced here with permission.

POINTS TO REMEMBER

- To help set the tone to prepare for learning, it may be helpful to have the whole class do Release before class and/or after recess.

- Doing Release can be a transitional activity between activities during the school day.

- Some learners can initially be self-conscious about making the 'hnnn' sound. Explain that, ultimately, they will be able to experience the same effect without doing the sigh. Explain that the vibrations from the vocal cords have an important part to play in how the feeling of Release is transmitted to the chest area.

- In the future, you can simply ask or remind a learner to 'do Release' whenever you notice holding, concentrating, tensing up, or 'over-trying'.

- Teach learners to do Release three times when angry, fearful, or frustrated in the classroom/playground.

- Use with individual learners when they are making comments such as, 'I'm tired,' or 'I don't want to do this anymore.'

- Use during testing.

Chapter 10: Picturing Words – Davis Symbol Mastery

When a subject-specific word is consistently causing confusion and disorientation in a learner, non-creative or passive teaching methods – such as explanations, recitations, and demonstrations – fail to stop the word from causing disorientations and mistakes. The learner will usually try to memorize or parrot what is being taught. Generally, we have found these teaching methods require a lot of repetition, are time-consuming, do not significantly address the meanings or concepts of a symbol, and have the potential to create additional confusion.

Davis Symbol Mastery is a creative, explorative approach to words that utilizes white reusable modeling clay and the learner's voice in order to bring together all three parts of a word in a single learning experience. As discussed in Part 1 of this book, the three parts of a word are:

- What it looks like
- What it sounds like
- What it means.

The Three Parts of a Word

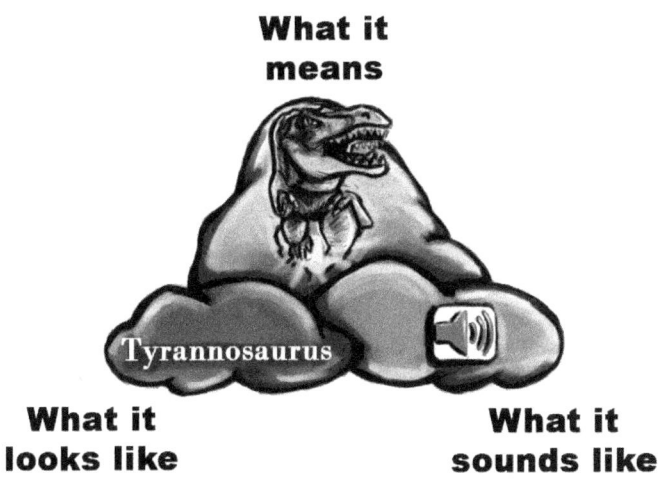

What it means

What it looks like

What it sounds like

The principles behind the technique are straightforward: the learner actively creates and experiences an association between all three elements of the word by

- creating a model showing what the word *means* (in agreement with the dictionary definition),
- creating what the written word *looks like*,
- *speaking* the word and its meaning out loud.

Modeling clay is used to create a model showing what the word means, and the letters needed to show what the written word looks like.

In a formal Davis program, this approach is usually preceded by a similar creative procedure for mastering basic language symbols such as letters and punctuation marks. This is particularly important when using the Davis methods to address difficulties with literacy, including dyslexia. Teachers wishing to explore this procedure can do so by purchasing a copy of *The Gift of Dyslexia* by Ronald Davis and/or by attending training workshops provided by their regional Davis Association.

Why Clay?

Creativity is an essential part of the learning process. When something has been learned so deeply that it becomes part of us, we say it has been mastered. Mastery requires creativity; the conscious active involvement of a learner.

If we create something in the form of memorization, that is what we have—something memorized. If we create something in the form of understanding, that's what we have—understanding. But if we create something in the form of mastery, it becomes a part of us: it becomes a part of our intellect. When something is mastered, it becomes a part of our thinking process.

No matter how often we watch someone riding a bicycle and understand what needs to be done, the understanding of it won't keep us from tipping over the first time we get on the bike. Mastering riding the bike requires that we get on the bike and ride it, experiencing

> it directly. We have to create the experience in the real world in order to master it.
>
> The question is: how can we master a word? We can't get on it and ride it around. But we can create it in the real world.
>
> When we make the meaning of the word in clay, what we are doing is creating its meaning in the real world.
>
> When we create the meaning of the word in clay, and then add what the word looks like and what the word sounds like, we have created the word in the real world. That word is mastered.
>
> – Ronald Davis

Getting Started with Symbol Mastery on Words

The Create-A-Word Exercise

This exercise introduces a learner to Symbol Mastery on Words in a creative and fun way. It establishes the idea that a word has three components:

1) what it looks like,

2) what it sounds like, and

3) what it means.

PROCEDURE

Note: If a learner is unfamiliar with shaping clay, take time first to demonstrate and practise making a three-dimensional shape, animal and human figure with clay.

Say to the learner:

1. Make something in clay that is totally your own invention or fantasy. It could be a machine, an idea, an action, a description, a strange animal, anything. (concept)

2. Give it a name that is a made-up name. (sound symbol)

3. Make that name in clay with the letters of the English alphabet; you can spell it any way you like. (letter symbol)

4. Tell the model its name and what it means.

5. Tell the word what it 'says' and how it is spelled.

The following is an example of a discussion with the learner that could follow on from this activity:

You have just created a word, a sound symbol and a written symbol that means the thing you first made in clay. You have mastered it, because you know what it means, what it sounds like, and what it's supposed to look like.

Of course, only you know what it means and how to say it properly, and how it's supposed to be spelt. Now, what if you wanted to teach the word to someone else? Just saying it to them or showing them the written word wouldn't be enough, would it? For them to really understand it, they would need to know what the letters and sounds you are using mean or represent, right?

Every language is composed of words that somebody made up. Just like you did in this exercise, they started with an idea or image that was in their mind, made a sound for it, and then created symbols that represented that sound. When a lot of people learned and agreed that that sound and those symbols would always mean the same thing, they could communicate verbally and in writing.

In English, we have words that already have sounds and letters that everybody has agreed upon. Their meanings and sounds are in the dictionary. With Symbol Mastery, you get to 'create' for yourself what those words mean, what they sound like, and what they look like. When you do this with words you have had difficulty using, spelling, reading, writing, or understanding, you will know and understand them the same way you know and understand your own created word.

Create-A-Word exercise and text © 1995 – 2004 Ronald D. Davis, *Gift of Dyslexia* Workshop Manual. Used with permission.

Davis Symbol Mastery Procedure for Words

The Davis Symbol Mastery® Procedure is a process that can be used to master any word that is causing confusion. As mentioned previously, the procedure brings the meaning, sound and appearance (spelling) of the word together in one place, with the direct involvement of the learner's own creativity. This places the word into the learner's long-term memory – or, we might even say, into his identity – so that he can think *with* that word in any field or discipline that requires it.

The first stage is to **look up the word**. Depending on the word, a dictionary, subject lexicon, textbook glossary or online resource may be appropriate for this purpose. Initially, you may need to guide the learner and teach the skill of looking up. Over time, you should enable your learner to become ever more independent in the look-up process.

Then, the learner should **say the word out loud**. Check first that your learner knows how to pronounce it. If not, you might speak the word yourself – but over time, guide your learner towards independence in finding out the pronunciation for himself. This could involve teaching the dictionary pronunciation key and/or using text-to-speech software. (Some online resources, such as www.dictionary.com, provide a little speaker icon which you can click to hear the word.)

Next, **the definition should be read out loud**. Where multiple definitions are provided, always select just one definition. See *Symbol Mastery Hints* below for further guidance on how to do this. If example sentences are given, these should be read out loud too, after the definition.

After this, **establish a clear understanding of the definition**. This is a brainstorming process that may involve discussion and further research. See *Symbol Mastery Hints* below for further guidance.

Once your learner can picture the meaning of the word in his mind, ask him to **make a clay model of the meaning described by the definition**. Once this is done, have your learner **make the word out of clay** and place it in front of the model. The word should be made in lower-case, print-style letters unless it normally begins with a capital letter.

The final stages get the learner to vocalize what has been done. Have your learner look at his model and say to it aloud, '**You are [*word*] meaning [*definition*]**. (E.g. 'You are *tension* meaning *the state of being stretched tight*.')

Then have your learner look at the clay word and say to it aloud, '**You say [*word*]**.' (E.g. 'You say *tension*.')

Finally, have your learner close his eyes and **make a mental image of the model and word** that have been made out of clay.

Depending on the educational purpose of the exercise, some or all of the following additional steps may be appropriate:

- Have your learner **touch the letters of the word and name each letter**, alternating backward and forward order until it is done fluently and confidently.
- Have your learner close his eyes and **spell the word backward and forward**. Beforehand, instruct your learner to peek whenever he can't picture the next letter clearly. Quickly intervene and insist on a peek whenever your learner shows signs of confusion. Continue until peeks are no longer needed.
- Have your learner **write the word**.
- Have your learner make up more sentences and phrases using the word. Alternatively, for subject-specific vocabulary, have him flick through a subject textbook, look for the word, and check for each instance found whether the meaning matches the definition that was modelled.

Prior to getting started on 'tricky' subject-specific vocabulary, mastering a familiar noun, adjective and verb can help a learner:

- to become familiar with the steps of the Symbol Mastery Procedure;
- to note the subtle differences between definitions of the same word;
- to learn how to model all the components of a word definition.

Figure 17: Symbol Mastery of puppy: *'a young dog'*

Further details of the Davis Symbol Mastery Procedure, including a nine-step summary chart of the process, can be found in *The Gift of Dyslexia* by Ronald Davis. See the back of this book for further information, both on Davis' book, and on training workshops provided by your regional Davis Association where the Symbol Mastery Procedure is demonstrated and practiced.

Symbol Mastery Hints for Subject-Specific Vocabulary

1. Some words have multiple definitions. Quickly identifying the definition pertaining to the subject material in question is a skill that requires practice. For example, the word *element* will typically have several definitions, only one of which will pertain to its meaning in chemistry. This definition will often be flagged by the inclusion of the word *chemistry* or *chemical* in brackets, just before the definition. Learning to scan the list of definitions to find key pointers of this kind will help you locate the required definition quickly.

2. If you hit a definition that you cannot make sense out of, there is probably a word in the definition you do not understand or have a meaning for. You can look up the confusing word, or look in another dictionary to see if it explains the definition more clearly. An electronic dictionary will often allow you to 'click through' to the definitions of words within the definition and will have a 'back button' that can then be used to return to the original word entry.

3. Make clay figures and models that are 'realistic.' This does not mean they have to be works of art, or precise to the finest detail. 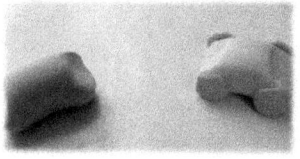 They should be three-dimensional, represent physical reality in a recognizable way, and not be overly abstract or symbolic. A lump of clay

cannot be representative of a car; the lump should at least have four wheels and be roughly the shape of a car.

4. A clay model of a person should be large enough and sturdy enough to stand on its own. A simple way of fashioning a clay person is to roll a cylinder of clay, cut vertical slits at each end, then manipulate the cut ends until they look like arms and  legs. A clay ball can then be fashioned into a head and placed on top of the torso. When you need to show action or emotion, the model should have arms and legs that can be positioned, and a head which can have facial expressions carved into it.

5. Make arrows out of clay to show directions or movement, sequence, or indicate a connection with another part of the model.

6. To show that something is an idea or in the mind, you can make a clay 'rope' into a 'cartoon bubble' that is attached to a person's head at one end. Form the other end of the rope into a loop, and lay the 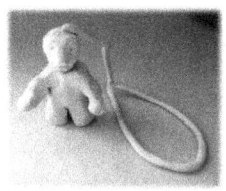 loop on the table. You can now place mini-models in the loop to show what is happening in the mind.

In a similar way, speech 'bubbles' can be used to show what a person is saying.

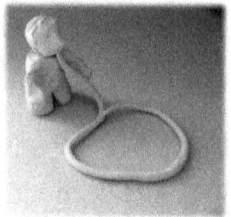

7. Make the clay letters of the words in lower case. They should be in a simple 'printed' form, resembling the way they would appear in books. Only begin a word with a capital letter if it is always capitalized (such as proper nouns and the pronoun *I*). Check to see that you have spelled the word correctly after you've made it in clay.

The good-looking but stupid soldier Pyrgopolynices is a central character in the Roman writer Plautus' comedy, *The Swaggering Soldier* (*Miles Gloriosus*)

8. If a definition seems hard or confusing, take a brief break. Look out a window, stand up for a minute, or just stretch your arms. Do the Release procedure.

9. Whether you are doing Symbol Mastery by yourself or helping someone else with it, make it a learning experience. Make it all right to make mistakes and get things wrong sometimes. Mistakes are one of the best ways to learn things.

10. Make Symbol Mastery a playful, fun, and game-like activity. Treat the words like little puzzles, and each definition as a piece or clue to that puzzle.

MASTERY TIPS

(for the final vocalized steps of the procedure)

* Make sure the learner only has the model and word in view when mastering.
* Encourage the learner to identify and point to each part of the definition represented by his model as the meaning is said.
* Encourage the learner to reflect on the accuracy of the modelled definition by asking 'What part of your model shows you …?'

Have fun!

Aggregate: a whole formed by combining several separate elements.
Source: Oxford Dictionary of English

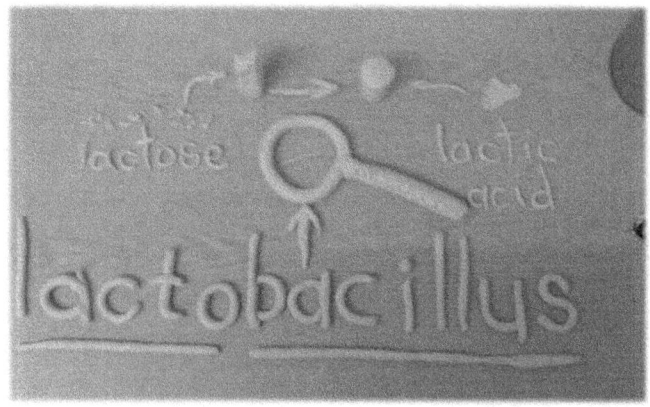

Lactobacillus: a rod-shaped bacterium which produces lactic acid and is widely distributed in milk.
Adapted from www.britannica.com

Why *Tyrannosaurus* But Not *If*?

As explained in Part 1 of this book, dyslexic learners frequently stumble on common connective words such as *as*, *the*, *when* and *if*. These two hundred or so words can disorient dyslexic individuals because their meaning is difficult to picture.

In a formal Davis program, learners are shown how to master these words using the Davis Symbol Mastery technique. For dyslexic individuals, mastery of these words is a key stepping-stone in the development of ease and accuracy in reading. Teachers wishing to find out more about this process can do so by purchasing a copy of *The Gift of Dyslexia* by Ronald Davis and/or by attending training workshops provided by their regional Davis Association.

Chapter 11: The End of the Reading Wars

Spell-Reading – Accurate, Analytical Reading for the Visual-Spatial Learner

In Chapter 5, we examined in some depth why recognition of the left-to-right sequence of letters in a word is a more fundamental reading skill than the ability either to decode phonically or to engage in whole-word recognition techniques. A word cannot be recognized with certainty if its individual components have not been recognized and processed. Logic dictates that accurate left-to-right recognition of the sequence of letters in a word is a necessary precursor to phonic decoding; one cannot decode the word *was*, for instance, if the mind is processing it as *saw*.

Spell-Reading, and the follow-on technique Sweep-Sweep-Spell, are a set of visual-spatial reading techniques from the Davis methods that together can reinforce accuracy of word recognition in readers who have not succeeded in doing so via traditional phonic routes. For other beginner readers, it can serve as a useful precursor to phonic instruction as it ensures that the learner's decoding abilities are built on a solid foundation of sequential letter recognition.

Two cards are placed over the book: one covering all lines below that which is being read, the other covering the right side of the line on which the student is working. In Spell-Reading, the helper moves the upper piece of card to reveal one letter at a time, while the student says the name (not the sound) of each letter out loud. When the end of the word is reached, the helper says the word and the reader repeats it. After a short while, the student can take control of the card, and if he knows the word straight away after he has read the final letter, he can say the word without waiting for the helper.

The helper's role is to ensure the student keeps to a steady pace, and promptly to supply any words not known by the student. This eliminates any need for the student to engage in guesswork. Guessing will prevent the feeling of certainty that a dyslexic student needs to in order to gain confidence in his reading ability.

Once the student is confident in the Spell-Reading technique and is recognising most of the words on his own, he can transition to the Sweep-Sweep-Spell stage. In this exercise, the student reveals a whole word at a time, 'sweeping' it from left to right with his eyes. If he recognises the word, he says it; if he does not, he re-covers it and sweeps it again. If he still does not recognise it after two sweeps, he reverts to Spell-Reading for that word, at the end of which the helper says the word and the reader repeats it.

A technical explanation of the theoretical basis behind these exercises can be found at http://www.dyslexia.com/articles/SERIOLandSpellReading.pdf For dyslexic learners, it is recommended that these techniques are applied in the context of the other Davis methods, as these will support their efficacy. Further detail of the techniques, and of their place in a formal Davis program, is available in *The Gift of Dyslexia* by Ronald Davis and at training workshops provided by Davis Associations.

*Important: sessions of Spell-Reading and Sweep-Sweep-Spell are **tiring** for the student. They should be limited to 5 minutes per session.*

Picture-At-Punctuation –
A Powerful Tool for Assimilating Facts in Reading

Picture-At-Punctuation is a simple Davis technique which enhances both comprehension and retention of what we read. The principles behind the technique are straightforward:

- Punctuation marks such as periods, exclamation points, question marks, colons, semicolons, and sometimes commas, mark the end of a complete thought;
- A complete thought can be either pictured or felt. The words: *'There was a woman standing by the...'* do not evoke a complete mental image. The complete

sentence: *'There was a woman standing by the kiosk.'* does;
- Words are but symbols. A word encodes an idea, but the idea itself is distinct from the word. To *comprehend* words or text, we have to *decode* them; consciously or unconsciously, we must convert the words that we read or hear into mental imagery;
- For detailed, conscious comprehension of text, the above punctuation marks serve as 'Stop Signs' where we can stop and check if we have a clear mental image (picture or feeling) about the sentence or clause we have just read.

Using this process for fictional text is an exciting process that brings the printed word to life. Try reading through the following passage that forms the opening of Franz Kafka's *Metamorphosis*, stopping at each vertical line to check your mental image of the section immediately preceding:

> **'As Gregor Samsa awoke one morning from uneasy dreams, | he found himself transformed in his bed into a gigantic insect. | He was lying on his hard, as it were armor-plated, back, | and when he lifted his head a little he could see his dome-like brown belly divided into stiff arched segments, | on top of which the bed quilt could hardly keep in position and was about to slide off completely. | His numerous legs, | which were pitifully thin compared to the rest of his bulk, | waved helplessly before his eyes.'**

Stopping at each period and most of the commas to create a conscious mental image converts this passage into a vivid, almost movie-like experience. As well as making reading pleasurable, the technique may enhance our critical reading abilities. Can insects actually lift their heads high enough to see their legs? Why does the passage refer to 'numerous legs' when all insects have just six?

Consciously converting words into images also enhances and extends our retention of what we read. I have worked with individuals who, after reading a passage using *Picture-At-Punctuation* just once, were able to answer comprehension questions on the passage, impromptu, in full detail as much as two weeks later.

So much for fictional writing; but what happens when a student applies this technique to factual texts, such as subject-specific reading for school? Take these passages:

> **'What is the impact of outward UK direct and portfolio investment? In the short term, overseas investment sees money leaving the country and so worsens the current account. In the long term, income earned from these UK assets owned overseas is a credit item in the income section of the current account. As a result of past overseas investment, the current account improves.'**[76]

---

[76] Source: Tutor2U - http://www.tutor2u.net/

'A mole of a molecular compound contains 6 x 10^{23} molecules. It has a mass that is equal to its relative formula mass. So a mole of water (H_2O) has a mass of 18 g. A mole of carbon dioxide (CO_2) has a mass of 44 g. This also works for ionic compounds, so a mole of sodium chloride (NaCl) has a mass of 58.5 g.'[77]

Without a certain level of subject knowledge, the *Picture-At-Punctuation* technique will seem to 'fail'. However, this is precisely the point at which the technique becomes a powerful diagnostic tool. If a student stops at a punctuation mark and cannot form a mental image, this tells us that one or more of the terms contained in the preceding sentence or clause is not fully comprehended by the student. For instance, if a student cannot picture the meaning of the words *outward*, *direct*, *portfolio* and/or *investment*, he or she will not succeed in creating a mental image for the meaning of the first question in the first passage. If a student cannot picture the meaning of *mole*, *molecule*, *compound*, *mass* and/or *relative formula mass*, he or she will make little headway in picturing the first two sentences of the second passage.

At this point, *Picture-At-Punctuation* can be used in conjunction with a range of simple research tools: discussion with a teacher or fellow-student, a paper or electronic dictionary, Internet resources including Google Images, and other Davis techniques such as Symbol

---

[77] Source: BBC Bitesize:
http://www.bbc.co.uk/education/guides/zysk7ty/revision/2

Mastery for Words, can all help to fill in the absent mental images for the meanings of these words. Doing so regularly with a student creates the habit of researching unknown words while reading. With this approach, *Picture-At-Punctuation* becomes not just an aid to reading comprehension, but a vehicle for repairing missing or mis-learnt knowledge.

> 'I am absolutely bursting with excitement, so had to drop you a note to let you know! Having read to W. this evening for half an hour he begged me to read another chapter. Being desperate for a cup of tea, I said to him that if he wanted to know what happened next he could read it himself – HE DID! ... he excitedly told me what had happened – so I know that he understood it as well! Thank you.'
>
> – *Mother of WY, aged 9 (reading Wolf Brother by Michael Paver). WY had recently undertaken a Davis Dyslexia Program with my wife Margarita.*

Stop Signs in Reading

Complete Stop	Short Stop	Pause
• period	; semicolon	, comma
! exclamation point	— dash	
? question mark		
: colon		

Copyright © 1996 by Ronald D. Davis. All rights reserved. Used with permission.

Chapter 12: Regular as Clockwork – A Creative Approach to Learning to Tell the Time

Some creative thinkers struggle to learn to tell the time. This linear, sequential, steady concept, together with the concepts of causality, measurement and counting that underpin it, can cause intractable problems for children with problems of attention focus and/or difficulties with mathematics. While most of these children eventually do learn to tell the time, it is often in a contrived and brittle manner that does not equate to full mastery. In later life, they may struggle with time management and punctuality because time as a concept never fully made sense.

Davis Concept Mastery is a clay-based process for mastering a range of concepts that include time, sequence, order and disorder. Prior to mastering these concepts, the learner masters the concepts of self, change, consequence, cause, effect, before, and after. Details of this process are provided in Ronald Davis' book, *The Gift of Learning* and at workshops provided by Davis Associates.

What follows here is a teaching module for explorative, creative mastery of the clock face. Though scripted as a one-to-one module, it can easily be adapted to a whole-class context. Rather than teach the clock face mechanistically, learners explore each fact, concept and skill that underpins the ability to tell the time. The approach is cross-curricular, drawing principally from Geography and Mathematics and, to a lesser extent, Physics and History. The result will be learners who *know* what they are *doing* when they read their timepieces.

It will take time to work through this full module, which may therefore run over several teaching sessions.

Equipment needed:

white reusable modeling clay, clay cutter, ruler, globe, flashlight, simple toy teaching clock

---

Important note: **The learning processes involved in this module are rich and intense. Have your learner use the Release Procedure frequently as needed. Take plenty of breaks. At any sign of frustration, *back off*, insist on a break, then resume the activity at an appropriate point prior to where the frustration started to occur.**

This is a long procedure, which you may want to spread over several sessions. Remember you are teaching a lifelong skill. Do not rush the process.

Measurement and standards as concepts within time

Length example

What to do	What to say
Roll out a short length of clay. (If working with a group of several learners, have them roll a short length of clay too.)	Here is a rope made of clay. How would you measure *how* long it is?
If the answer 'a ruler' or 'a tape measure' is not forthcoming, supply this information. Get out a real classroom ruler. (If working with a group, supply one for each learner or pair of learners.) As required, guide your learner(s) towards laying the rope alongside the ruler.	
Briefly discuss the units of	Look at the markings on

length shown on the ruler.*	the ruler. Do you know what they are called?
	Would the ruler work if it were made of elastic? Why not?

* Note: the following script makes use of the millimeter and centimeter markings on the ruler. If your learner is more familiar with inches and feet, adapt the procedure accordingly.

<u>Units of measurement</u>

What to do	**What to say**
On the ruler, have the learner count how many millimeters there are in a centimeter. Establish that there are 10 millimeters in every centimeter.	
Say:	Therefore, millimeters and centimeters are part of the same system of measurement. We call them *units of measurement.*

155

Establish that we usually choose the unit most convenient for the size of what we are measuring. If appropriate for the learner's age and maturity, discuss meters and kilometers as units for measuring longer lengths and distances.	Would it be convenient to measure your height in millimeters? Why not? What about the distance from here to your home?

<u>Introduction to standards</u>

What to do	**What to say**
All the units so far discussed originate from the meter standard. The origin of the meter standard as one ten millionth of the distance from the North Pole to the Equator can be of great interest to some learners.	
(See http://physics.nist.gov/cuu/Units/meter.html for some further factual detail.)	
If your learner expresses	

interest, you can also explore how other standards were derived from the meter standard (one gram is the mass of one cubic centimeter of water; one liter is the space occupied by 1,000 cubic centimeters of water).	
Establish that your learner understands that you cannot measure one phenomenon (e.g. mass) with a unit of measurement expressing another phenomenon (e.g. length).	Could you measure your mass/weight in meters? Why not?

Measurement of change: the day standard

What to do	**What to say**
Have your learner think of a simple example of a change that would take less than a day to complete. (E.g. baking a loaf of bread). Have your learner make a model of the change out of clay, or draw a picture of it. This will	

ensure the change stays in your learner's awareness as you continue with the next steps.	
Discuss how we measure change.	What instrument(s) would we use to measure this change?
If your learner doesn't immediately understand, rephrase and ask:	What instrument(s) we would use to measure how long this change takes?
In response, your learner should name a timepiece such as a clock/watch/stopwatch.	

<u>Units and standard of change measurement</u>

What to do	**What to say**
	What units do we find on a [timepiece previously named by the learner]?
Discuss how seconds fit exactly into minutes (x 60) and minutes	

into hours (x 60).	
Your learner should respond: 'a day'. If not, supply the information and discuss.	What unit is the next one up? What do hours fit exactly into?

The day standard

What to do	**What to say**
Discuss how the times of day reflect the real processes of day and night.	Would it be a good idea to go for a picnic at midnight? Why not?
Elicit the response from your learner: 'It is dark'.	
	Is it always dark at midnight?
Your learner should respond 'yes'. But does your learner know why? As needed, proceed to explore the answer with a globe and flashlight (see next section).	

The day standard: globe-and-flashlight demonstration

Note: even better than a flashlight is a modern round table lamp or orb, if available.

What to do	What to say
Place a small piece of clay on the globe, on the approximate place where the session with your learner is taking place (e.g. two-thirds of the way up the east coast of the USA if the session is taking place in New York).	
Darken the room.	
Have your learner switch on the flashlight and point it directly at one side of the globe. The flashlight represents the sun.	
Discuss with your learner which direction on the globe is east.	
Discuss with your learner that, first thing in the morning, we see the sun in the east of the sky.	This is called 'sunrise'.

Instruct your learner to turn the globe to show the earth's position when it is sunrise in the place marked by the piece of clay.	
	Can you now work out which way the earth spins?
Give assistance as needed.	
Have your learner turn the globe (in the 'right' direction) and explore how the earth is positioned in relation to the sun when, at the place marked with clay, it is: o *midday;* o *mid-afternoon;* o *early evening / sunset;* o *midnight;* o *etc.*	
When this has been thoroughly explored, ask:	How long does it take for the earth to make one full rotation?
Assist with further discussion as needed.	

	Does the earth speed up and slow down as it turns, or does it turn at a constant speed?
	Why is this important in order that the earth's rotation can serve as a time standard?
If appropriate, discuss again why a ruler would not work if it were made of elastic (see above). Compare this (hypothetically) to an earth which changed speed as it turned.	
If your learner is well-travelled, and/or has relatives elsewhere in the world, and seems interested, you could explore time zones. E.g. what time of day (roughly) is it in the UK when it is midday in New York?	

Divisions of the day

What to do	What to say
With the globe still on the table, discuss how an hour is one twenty-fourth of a day.	
Show your learner how to make a slight anti-clockwise turn of the earth, approximating to 1/24 of a rotation.	What you have just done is what an hour means. That is what the earth does during an hour.
Have the learner make a large ball out of clay to represent the earth (including a still larger ball representing the sun, and showing the earth's tilt).	
*Discuss the concept of a **meridian**: an imaginary arc on the Earth's surface from the North Pole to the South Pole. If the learner does not assimilate the concept readily and with certainty, master using the **Davis Symbol Mastery** procedure.*	
Have the learner use the Davis Symbol Mastery procedure to	

make separate models for:
 	
   o **midday**: *the time when the local meridian directly faces the sun*
   o **midnight**: *the opposite of midday.*
 	
Keep the models nearby.	

The clock face – the hour hand

What to do	**What to say**
Have the learner make a simple but fairly large clay disc to represent a clock face. Have the learner make just the hour hand. Ascertain if the learner knows the following, supplying information as needed:	Which direction does the hour hand go? How many hours are there in a day? How long (as a fraction of a day) does it take for the hour hand to make a full rotation? How much does the earth rotate while this happens?

*Discuss with the learner how both midday and midnight are called 'twelve o'clock'. Check the learner is familiar with the word **o'clock**; clarify/master as needed.*	
*Have the learner make and place '12.00' underneath the models for **midday** and **midnight** and repeat the vocal steps of Davis Symbol Mastery to re-master them ('You are twelve o'clock, meaning the time where the local meridian…').*	
Have the learner place the numerals '12' in the correct position on the clay clock (give guidance as needed).	
Using the globe and flashlight, explore where the local meridian is, in relation to the sun, at 6.00.	
Discuss how 6.00 occurs twice in the course of a day, and discuss/ explore how one of the occurrences is in the early	

morning (around dawn) and the other in the early evening (around dusk).	
Have the learner place the numeral '6' in the correct position on the clay clock.	
Repeat this process for 3.00 and 9.00.	
Add the remaining numbers to the clay clock. Place the hour hand at 12.00. Say:	This means that it's 12.00. It takes *one hour* for this hand to go from one number to the next. Where will it be one hour from now?
Have learner move hour hand to 1.00. Say:	So now it's one o'clock. Where will the hour hand be, not one hour, but *half an hour* from now?
Have the learner move the hour hand to half way between 1 and 2. Say:	We call this time **half past one**.
Have the learner do Davis Symbol Mastery on: ○ **past**: beyond in time	

REGULAR AS CLOCKWORK – A CREATIVE APPROACH TO LEARNING TO TELL THE TIME

Ask the learner:	Where will it be in another half an hour?
Have the learner move the (hour) hand to point to 2.	
Ask:	Where will it be in a quarter of an hour?
Have the learner move the hand a quarter of the way between 2 and 3. Say:	We call this time **a quarter past two**.
Ask:	Where will it be in another quarter of an hour?
*Have the learner move the hand to half of the way between 2 and 3. See if the learner can name this time as **half past two**.*	
Ask:	Where will it be in another quarter of an hour?
Have the learner move the hand three quarters of the way between 2 and 3. Say:	We call this time **a quarter to three**.
Have the learner do Davis	

Symbol Mastery on: ○ ***to**: approaching in time*	
Continue to discuss where the hour hand will be at various other times involving 'o'clock', 'half past', 'a quarter past' and 'a quarter to' (e.g. 'a quarter past five', 'a quarter to nine', 'half past four', 'ten o'clock', etc.)	

The clock face – the minute hand

What to do	**What to say**
On the toy teaching clock, point out the hour hand, the minute hand, and the minute markings.	
Discuss why the minute hand is longer (so that it 'reaches' the minute markings around the edge).	

REGULAR AS CLOCKWORK –
A CREATIVE APPROACH TO LEARNING TO TELL THE TIME

Position the hour and minute hand so they both point at 12. Say:	The minute hand and hour hand move at the same time, but the minute hand moves faster.
Say:	It takes one hour for the hour hand to move from one number to the next; but while it does that, the minute hand travels right round the clock.
Demonstrate what you have just said by moving the minute hand right round the clock face while you, more slowly, move the hour hand just one hour setting.	
If desired/appropriate, show the online clock at http://www.visnos.com/demos/clock Allow your learner to rotate the hour hands and minute hands by clicking and dragging on the end of each hand in turn; see how the other hand moves at the same time.	
Ask:	Show where the two hands will be in an hour. (Answer: 1.00.)
Ask:	Show where the two hands will be in half an

	hour. (1.30).
Continue with quarter-hours.	
Discuss impossible times. (e.g. hour hand pointing directly at 1, while minute hand is pointing at 6. Can the learner explain why this is impossible?)	
Explore 'five past', 'ten past', etc. Discuss/explain that each number on the clock represents 5 minutes (because 60 ÷ 12 = 5).	
If desired/appropriate, let the learner play online games such as that at http://www.visnos.com/demos/clock	

Going Further: Calendar Mastery

Some learners also find it difficult to remember the sequence of the months of the year. This may go hand in hand with limited awareness of the sequence of the seasons, and why the seasons occur.

The following additional procedure can be undertaken to explore the seasons and master the order of the months of the year.

Remember: **Have your learner use the Release Procedure frequently as needed. Take plenty of breaks. At any sign of frustration, *back off*, insist on a break, then resume the activity at an appropriate point prior to where the frustration started to occur.**

<u>Measurement of change: the year standard</u>

What to do	What to say
Have your learner think of a change that takes several months to occur (e.g. a seedling growing into a plant).	
Guide your learner towards understanding that rather than a clock, you would use a calendar.	Would you use a clock to measure this change? What would you use instead?

<u>The year standard and the cycle of seasons: globe-and-flashlight demonstration</u>

Note: even better than a flashlight is a modern round table lamp or orb, if available.

*Useful background information: when the north pole is facing towards the observer, the earth rotates around the sun in an **anti-clockwise** direction.*

What to do	What to say
Make sure that the piece of clay is still on the globe, marking the place where the teaching session is taking place.	
Darken the room again.	
Stand with your learner in an area of the room where there is plenty of space for you to walk around your learner during the demonstration.	
Have your learner switch on the flashlight and point it directly at the globe. The flashlight represents the sun.	
Hold the globe with the tilt so positioned that the North Pole faces away from the 'sun'. Spin the earth on its axis and keep it spinning for the rest of the demonstration.	

Discuss which half of the earth (hemisphere) is getting longer days and more sun. Guide your learner to understand that this is midwinter in the northern hemisphere and midsummer in the southern hemisphere. It is December. (Learners in the northern hemisphere may be surprised to hear that, in South Africa / Australia / New Zealand, Christmas can be celebrated on the beach!)	

Important: you are about to start walking around your learner in an anti-clockwise direction. As you do so, keep the north pole tilted in the same direction **in relation to the room,** *not in relation to the sun. For instance, if you start with the north pole tilted towards the door, keep the north pole tilted towards the door throughout the demonstration. For more background information on why this is, see https://en.wikipedia.org/wiki/Pole_star If you do not adhere to this instruction, you will not be able to demonstrate to your learner what makes the seasons occur.*

What to do	What to say
While still spinning the earth on its axis, walk one quarter-turn round your learner in an anti-clockwise direction.	
Show and discuss how the northern and southern hemispheres are now getting equal amounts of sun and daylight. (If appropriate, you can introduce the concept of equinox).	
Include the following:	This is where the earth is in March. It is spring in the north and autumn in the south.
While still spinning the earth on its axis, walk another quarter-turn round your learner in an anti-clockwise direction.	
Discuss which half of the earth (hemisphere) is now getting longer days and more sun. Guide your learner to understand that this is midsummer in the northern	

hemisphere and midwinter in the southern hemisphere. It is June.	
While still spinning the earth on its axis, walk another quarter-turn round your learner in an anti-clockwise direction.	
Show and discuss how, just as in March, the northern and southern hemispheres are now getting equal amounts of sun and daylight.	
Include the following:	This is where the earth is in September. It is autumn in the north and spring in the south.
While still spinning the earth on its axis, walk one quarter-turn round your learner in an anti-clockwise direction. Discuss with your learner that it is now December again, and the earth is in the place where it was when you started the demonstration.	

Ask:	Therefore, how long does it take for the earth to complete a full orbit around the sun? (Answer: one year.)

Mastering the order of the months of the year

You will need a (very) large table or floor mat. Have your learner make a large ball out of clay and place it in the center of the table or mat. Explain to your learner that this ball represents the sun.

Have your learner make 12 smaller balls. Explain to your learner that these balls represent the earth at different points in its orbit around the sun.

Have your learner draw a line around each of the earth-balls. Explain to your learner that this line represents the *equator*. Explain the concept of the equator as needed. If your learner still seems uncertain of the concept after your explanation, allow him/her to master it using Davis Symbol Mastery and an appropriate dictionary definition.

Have your learner place two dabs of clay on each earth-ball, where the north and south poles would be. Explain the concepts of *north pole* and *south pole* as needed. If your learner still seems uncertain of the concepts after your explanation, allow him/her to master them using Davis Symbol Mastery and an appropriate dictionary definition.

Have your learner poke a little hole on each earth-ball, in the approximate place where the teaching session is taking place. (E.g. if in New York, the hole is poked about mid-way between the equator and the north pole).

Have your learner arrange all 12 balls with the north pole inclined toward a specific end of the room (in these instructions, we will assume the end containing the door). Agree with your learner a 'rule' that, in all subsequent movements of the balls, the north pole must always incline towards the door. Be alert to any violations; as needed, gently remind the learner of the rule.

Have your learner place one of the earth-balls on the mat, on what would be a line between the sun-ball and the door. Ensure your learner continues to observe the 'rule'. This will mean that the north pole is tilted away from the sun. Discuss which half of the earth (hemisphere) is getting longer days and more sun. Guide your learner to understand that this is midwinter in the northern hemisphere and midsummer in the southern hemisphere. Explain that this represents December; have your learner make the word *December* out of clay and place it directly under the earth-ball.

Have your learner place one of the earth-balls on the mat, on what would be a line between the sun-ball and the wall opposite the door. Ensure your learner continues to observe the 'rule'. This will mean that the north pole is tilted towards the sun. Discuss which half of the earth (hemisphere) is getting longer days and more sun. Guide your learner to understand that this is midsummer in the northern hemisphere and midwinter in the southern hemisphere. Explain that this represents June; have your learner make the word *June* out of clay and place it directly under the earth-ball.

Repeat the same process for *March* and *September*. Use the photograph below if you need guidance as to the balls' positions. Ensure your learner continues to observe the 'rule'. This will mean that the tilt of the earth is perpendicular to the sun.

Repeat the same process for all the remaining months. Use the photograph below if you need guidance as to the balls' positions. Ensure your learner continues to observe the 'rule'.

Starting at January, have your learner look at and touch each of the earth-balls in turn, naming the month while doing so. Ensure your learner is doing so in a forward direction ('January – February – March', etc.)

Starting at December, have your learner look at and touch each of the earth-balls in turn, naming the month while doing so. Ensure your learner is doing so in a backward direction ('December – November – October', etc.)

Name a month at random. Have your learner locate the month, touch the appropriate earth-ball, then name the month before and after it. (E.g. if you say 'June', your learner should touch the June earth-ball and say 'May – July'.) Repeat the process until you have named every month, in random order.

Have your learner close her eyes and create a mental image of what she has created. Have your learner name each month in forward order with eyes closed; explain that she should be guided by her mental image and should take a peek whenever she cannot picture the next month clearly. Be alert to any signs of effort or guesswork; intervene immediately and insist on a peek whenever such signs occur.

Have your learner close her eyes and repeat the above process, this time naming the months in backward order, taking peeks whenever needed.

Have your learner continue to alternate forward and backward, taking peeks whenever needed, until the need for peeking ceases. Ensure the final naming session is in forward order. Celebrate the success!

(Note: the vertical line in the middle of the image is a join in the table – it is not an integral part of the model!)

Chapter 13: Place Value

Some creative learners struggle to master mathematical concepts and processes. In many cases, this is because the concepts underlying mathematical knowledge have not been fully understood and/or because the child was progressed too quickly from real-world manipulatives onto paper-based techniques that utilize mathematical symbols without showing their meaning. For example, some children attempt to rote-learn the multiplication tables without really understanding that multiplication is adding in groups. They cannot therefore picture what multiplication means, nor what is happening to the quantities represented by the numerals when multiplication is occurring. As a result, their knowledge of multiplication will be fragile, and their knowledge of division as a permutation of multiplication will be close to non-existent.

The Davis Math Mastery Program is a systematic, multisensory approach to the building of basic arithmetical proficiency. The concepts underlying mathematical knowledge and the processes of arithmetic are explored through the medium of clay, utilizing clay balls as real quantities, before the learner transitions to paper-based mathematics and to working with mathematical symbols. Details of this process are provided in Ronald Davis' book, *The Gift of Learning* and at workshops provided by Davis Associates.

The module scripted below can serve as a multisensory way of teaching place value. A firm understanding of place value is fundamental to all arithmetic beyond single-digit addition and subtraction.

Equipment needed:

100 balls made out of white reusable modeling clay (you might make these together with your learner at the start of the session), further clay, clay cutter

Important note: **The learning processes involved in this module are rich and intense. Have your learner use the Release Procedure frequently as needed. Take plenty of breaks. At any sign of frustration, *back off*, insist on a break, then resume the activity at an appropriate point prior to where the frustration started to occur.**

The initial Numeral Mastery sequence will be of benefit to many learners. If you are sure that your learner has mastered basic numerals *and* can picture the quantities that they represent, this sequence could be omitted or abbreviated.

Numeral Mastery

Issue the learner with a strip of paper that shows the numerals from 0 – 9 in a simple print style. If helpful, blow up the strip below on a photocopier and cut it out:

0 1 2 3 4 5 6 7 8 9

Take two clay balls and place them above the numeral 2 on the strip. Explain to your learner that the numeral 2 is a symbol that represents the quantity shown by the two balls. As needed, explain the same principle with the other numerals. Ensure your learner understands that the numeral 0 represents nothing.

Have your learner make the numerals from 0 – 9 and place the appropriate quantity of balls above each numeral. Ensure that your learner realizes there should be nothing above the numeral 0.

Have your learner look at each numeral and quantity, touch the quantity, and say the number, going forward from 0 – 9.

Have your learner look at each numeral and quantity, touch the quantity, and say the number, going backward from 9 – 0.

Have your learner look at each numeral and quantity, without touching, and say the number, going forward from 0 – 9.

Have your learner look at each numeral and quantity, without touching, and say the number, going backward from 9 – 0.

Have your learner name each number in forward order with eyes closed; explain that he should be guided by his mental image and should take a peek whenever he cannot picture the next number clearly. Be alert to any signs of effort or guesswork; intervene immediately and insist on a peek whenever such signs occur.

Have your learner close his eyes and repeat the above process, this time naming the numbers in backward order, taking peeks whenever needed.

Have your learner continue to alternate forward and backward, taking peeks whenever needed, until the need for peeking ceases.

Place Value

Do	Say
Have the learner clear away all the numerals and quantities except for 9. Have the learner move 9 (the numeral and quantity) to a space a little to the right of the center of the table.	
Point to the 9 balls.	This is the largest quantity that can be represented by a single numeral symbol. Does that make sense?
Throw a 10*th* ball in amidst the 9 balls.	I have now created disorder. We can't create order here (point to the place where the balls are) because there is no single numeral symbol that can represent this quantity.
Instruct the learner in forming the 10 balls into a cluster consisting of a base made out of 6 balls (arranged 3 x 2) and a top made out of 4 balls (2 x 2).	

PLACE VALUE

Point to a space a little to the learner's left from the 9 and the cluster. Let the learner leave the 9 numeral in place for now. *Make another 10-cluster. Place it, and a clay ball, in your area of the table.*	Move this cluster of 10 balls to here.
Point to the place where the 10-cluster has been put.	We can now create order. This is the place where we will count these (pick up your 10-cluster and show it to the learner). Not individual '1's, but these (once again show the learner the 10-cluster).
Point to the empty space above the 9 numeral, where the 9 balls had previously been.	This is still the place where we count these (pick up the individual ball and show it to the learner).

If appropriate, you could introduce the term 'units' here instead of '1's.	So let's create order with the numerals now. This (point to the numeral 9) is disorder, isn't it? What numeral do you need to place here instead, to show how many '1's there are here?
The learner should remove the numeral 9 and put the numeral 0 in its place.	
	That is correct. And what numeral do you need to place here (point to the space below the 10-cluster), to show how many of these (point to the 10-cluster) there are here? Not how many individual '1's; how many of these (point again to the 10-cluster).
The learner should place the numeral 1 below the 10-cluster.	
	That is correct. So this is why we write 10 as a '1'

PLACE VALUE

	and a '0': the numerals are showing that there is one of these (point to the 10-cluster) and no individual '1's.
Write '12' on a piece of paper. Show it to the learner.	How would you show '12' in the same way?
The learner should leave the 10-cluster and the numeral 1 in place, remove the numeral 0, place 2 balls in the units area and place the numeral 2 below it.	
	That is correct.
Repeat the process with further numbers between 13 and 99. Do as many examples as needed until the learner can confidently show the quantity and numeral in each case.	
Write '99' on a piece of paper.	Make 99 in the same way. I can help you if you like.
If you do help to make the clusters, keep back the 10-	

cluster and the individual ball you placed on your side of the table earlier.	
When the learner has made 99 – the numerals and the quantity – playfully throw an extra ball in amidst the 9 units.	
	I have created disorder. Can you create order?
The learner should form a 10-cluster out of the 10 balls and move it to the place where the 9 existing 10-clusters are arranged. The learner may well notice the problem with this.	
	Now there is disorder in the 10s' area, because you have ten 10-clusters and we don't have a numeral symbol to show any quantity greater than 9. So how can you create order?
See if the learner can work out that he/she needs to cluster all the 10-clusters	

PLACE VALUE

together into a 100-cluster and move it one space to his/her left. Give guidance as needed. Let the learner leave the numerals '99' in place for now.	
	Now make order with the numerals. This is the place where you count these (point to the 100-cluster). How many of these do you have here?
Elicit the answer '1'.	Place the numeral here (point to the space below the 100-cluster) that shows this.
	This is the place where you count these (point to your 10-cluster that you made earlier). How many of these are there here? (Point to the empty space above the '9' numeral in the tens column.
Elicit the answer 'zero' / 'naught' / 'none'. Guide the learner to replace the	

numeral 9 with the numeral 0.	
	This is the place where you count these (point to the individual ball on your side of the table). How many of these are there here? (Point to the empty space above the '9' numeral in the units column.
Elicit the answer 'zero' / 'naught' / 'none'. Guide the learner to replace the numeral 9 with the numeral 0.	
If appropriate to the learner's maturity and interest, invite him/her to imagine what the following quantities would look like: • 200 • 900 • 999	

Ask the learner if he/she can visualize what would happen if one ball were added to 999. Have the learner talk you through the steps that would be involved to create order, ending with a 1000 cluster in the 1000s' column. Briefly discuss what a 10,000 and a 100,000 cluster would look like.	

Chapter 14: Chemistry – Introducing Moles

Arguably, moles are one of the most elusive concepts that high school pupils of chemistry are required to master. They only make sense if key elements of atomic theory and bonding have been thoroughly mastered. They pre-suppose a solid grounding in mathematical principles. And above all, they are mind-blowingly large – or atoms are mind-blowingly tiny, depending on which way you look at it. A mole – 6.02×10^{23} of a particular atom, molecule or other elementary unit – is a number too vast to visualize. A modern 1080p television screen contains just over two million pixels. To assemble a mole of pixels, you would need more than 300,000,000,000,000,000 TVs. Unfortunately, there aren't anywhere near that many TVs on the planet.

Because the knowledge required to understand moles is so multi-layered, some learners may require a solid, multisensory learning experience in order to render that understanding permanent. Often, teachers of chemistry will find that children who seemed to 'get' the concept in

Ninth Grade, getting most of their mole calculations right, will return to the topic in Tenth or Eleventh Grade with only the faintest recollection of what it is all about. In particular, they may fail to understand why moles are useful when predicting the products of a reaction.

Taking and adapting the principles of Davis Symbol Mastery, it is possible to create a teaching module that helps anchor the meaning of moles for good. I have conducted this module successfully with a number of early high school age learners.

Step 1: What is an atom, and what is it made of?

Make sure your learner understands what is an atom, and what are its basic particles. Use dictionaries, google images and clay modelling as appropriate. In particular, make sure your learner understands that a proton and a neutron have equal mass, and that the mass of an electron is so small by comparison as to be negligible (i.e. you can ignore its mass, just as you would ignore the mass of a fly on the windscreen when calculating the mass of a car).

Make sure your learner understands the difference between *atomic number* (the number of protons in an atom) and *mass number* (the number of protons and neutrons taken together). Check that your learner understands that, because a proton and a neutron are equal in mass, each can be thought of as an atomic mass unit. See if your learner can explain why it wouldn't be practical to calculate the mass of an atom in grams (because the answer would be a tiny number with many 0s after the decimal point).

Make sure your learner understands what an *element* is – referring to a dictionary as needed. Look together at the periodic table, pointing out how the atomic number and mass number are given for each element. (If you need to explain why the mass number is usually not a whole number, you will need to conduct a session on isotopes and relative atomic mass before moving on.)

Step 2: A mole is a (very big) number

Discuss what Avogadro's constant – 6.02×10^{23} – actually means. Work out together how to write it out in long form as 602,000,000,000,000,000,000,000[78]. There are some well-designed videos on Youtube which illustrate what this number means: for instance, that a mole of tennis balls would be the size of a planet.

Step 3: Making an atom

Have your learner make a clay model depicting an atom of a particular element. Lithium works well: a lithium atom contains 3 protons and 4 neutrons in the

---

[78] This is a working approximation. The precise version would be 602,214,085,774,000,000,000,000.

nucleus and 3 electrons in the orbital shells. Remind your learner that the electrons do not contribute to the atom's mass because they are so tiny.

Calculate together the mass number of the atom, in atomic mass units (amu). For lithium, the mass will be 7 amu. Have your learner make the letters '7 amu' out of clay and place them under the model of the atom.

Have your learner make a magnifying glass out of clay and place it around the atom. Explain that this indicates that the atom is much, much smaller than the model. If appropriate, explain that, in fact, an atom is too small to show up in any magnifier or microscope that has yet been invented, so the magnifying glass here is used symbolically.

Step 4: Making a mole

Have your learner make a container out of clay. This could be a bag, a box or a pot, for example. Have your learner make a set of scales out of clay – modern digital-display scales work well – and place the container on the scales.

Have your learner make a long rope of clay with an arrowhead on one end. Have your learner place the resulting long arrow to go from the atom (not the magnifying glass) to the container. Have your learner write 'x 6.02×10^{23}' on a post-it note. Have your learner place the post-it note part-way along the arrow. Discuss that this means the container contains 6.02×10^{23} atoms of the kind that has been modelled. As necessary, discuss that the container itself is symbolic and 'weightless'.

Have your learner write on another post-it note the mass of the mole in grams. If the atom used was a lithium atom (with a mass of 7 amu), the mass of the mole will be 7g. Have your learner place the post-it note on the scales, representing its digital display.

Finally, have your learner make the word 'mole' and place it under the model. Discuss with your learner what has been made, and then ask her to explain it back to you.

Have your learner look away or close her eyes and make a clear mental image of what she has created.

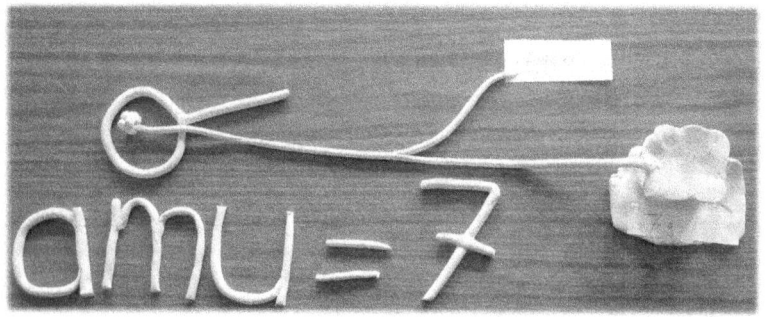

Discuss with your learner how the atoms of different elements have different masses. Discuss the mass of a mole of various elements and its relationship with the element's mass number. For instance, find lead (Pb) on the periodic table. Establish that its mass number is 207 amu. Tell your learner that a mole of lead has a mass of

207g. Find calcium (Ca) on the periodic table. Establish that its mass number is 40 amu. Tell your learner that a mole of calcium has a mass of 40g. Continue with similar examples until your learner realizes that the mass of a mole of an element is the same number of grams as the number of amu in the mass of a single atom. Allow your learner to verbalize this; explore further examples to ensure your learner can predict the mass of a mole from the element's mass number.

Going Further

As and when appropriate, explore the molar mass of compounds. Naturally, this will require prior exploration of ionic and covalent bonding, of elementary particles, and of relative formula mass. As necessary, have your learner make further clay models illustrating how the molar mass of a compound relates to the compound's relative formula mass.

When exploring mole calculation exercises with your learner, have her visualize her mental image of her clay model and retell its components, as needed, as you go along.

Chapter 15: Pulling it All Together

So how do we pull together everything learnt and discussed in this book, so that our classrooms become truly 'friendly' to all of our learners – the at-risk ones, the scholarly ones, the practical ones, the artistic ones, the sporty ones – how do we accommodate all their diverse needs in the single curriculum that we have to teach?

Even for those of you who teach mainstream classes with few struggling learners, consider how their needs may be utilized to enhance the learning of all your pupils. A classroom geared to non-dyslexic learners will not be friendly to the dyslexic learner. However, a classroom designed to be 'dyslexia-friendly' does not become unfriendly to the non-dyslexic learner. It does not become slower-paced, more repetitive or intellectually less rigorous. It simply becomes more experiential. When crafted with care, experiential learning can be to the benefit of all.

These are the key features of a dyslexia-friendly learning environment:

- Whenever possible, information gets tested so it can be experienced as true;
- Teachers are alert to signs of confusion in their learners, and react appropriately to them;
- Learners can be responsible for managing their inner state, through a range of self-management tools;
- Curricular material is sequentially ordered to maximise certainty and minimise confusion;
- Whenever possible, material is explored rather than memorised.

To illustrate these principles in action, let us return to the opening example of this book in order to paint two pictures of two different learning scenarios.

Two different classes are learning the word 'because'. In one class, the teacher teaches the children an acrostic: 'Big Elephants Cannot Always Use Small Exits'. The opening chapter of this book recounts vividly what happened to one little boy when this approach was taken.

In the other classroom, the teacher places a banana skin on the floor, walks over it and pretends to slip. 'Why did I slip?' he asks the class. 'Because there was a banana skin there', they reply.

The scene is now set to explore the law of cause and effect. If desired, the class could also explore the relationship between this law and the flow of time

('Which came first: the person dropping the banana skin or me walking across the floor? If it had been the other way around, would I have slipped?')

The teacher then asks each child to think up his or her own sentence incorporating 'because'. Time permitting, the class could then master 'because' using Davis Symbol Mastery. Finally, the pupils could close their eyes, spell the word forward and backward (a good technique for visual-spatial anchoring) and then see how many instances of the word they can find in written material.

The first teacher got through the material more quickly. Yet how many students of his pupils will have fully learnt 'because'?

The second teacher spent more time and also taught the meaning of 'because'. How likely is it that she will have to come back to the word to reinforce it?

Not every teaching situation affords the time to go into such experiential depth around a single word. Every teacher has to set priorities for the limited teaching time that they have. But if we have clear insight into the value that experiential mastery brings to a learning process, this insight alone will make us a more precious resource for our learners than we would otherwise be.

> 'When someone masters something, it becomes a part of that person. It becomes part of the individual's thought and creative process. It adds the quality of its essence to all subsequent thought and creativity of the individual.'
>
> – Ronald Davis, author, *The Gift of Dyslexia*, *The Gift of Learning*.

Bibliography

Additude, 2006. *What Is a 'Slow Processing Speed?'*. [Online]
Available at: http://www.additudemag.com/q%26a/ask_the_learning_expert/1553.html
[Accessed 29 July 2016].

Ariely, D., 2008. *Predictably Irrational.* New York: HarperCollins.

Ashcraft, M. H. & Jeremy, A. K., 2007. Working memory, math performance, and math anxiety. *Psychonomic Bulletin & Review,* 14(2), pp. 243-248.

Associated Press, 1995. *UK: Prime Minister John Major Local Elections Comment.* [Online]
Available at: http://www.aparchive.com/
[Accessed 05 08 2015].

Baddeley, A. & Hitch, G. J., 1974. Working memory. In. *The psychology of learning and motivation: Advances in research and theory,* Volume 8, pp. 47-89.

British Broadcasting Corporation, 2017. *Independent school students gain extra time for exams.* [Online]
Available at: http://www.bbc.co.uk/news/education-38923034
[Accessed 16 April 2017].

British Dyslexia Association, 2015. *Literacy Tuition.* [Online]
Available at:
http://www.bdadyslexia.org.uk/educator/literacy-tuition
[Accessed 21 October 2015].

British Dyslexia Association, 2015. *Visual Stress.* [Online]
Available at:
http://www.bdadyslexia.org.uk/dyslexic/eyes-and-dyslexia
[Accessed 21 October 2015].

Brown, E. N., 2009. *Meaning, Morphemes and Literacy: Essays in the Morphology of Language and Its Application to Literacy.* Kibworth(Leicestershire): Book Guild Publishing.

Cavanna, A. E. & Trimble, M. R., 2006. The precuneus: a review of its functional anatomy and behavioural correlates. *Brain,* Volume 129, pp. 564-583.

Centre for Reading and Language, 2009. *The North Yorks Reading Intervention Project,* York: Centre for Reading and Language.

Chamberlain, R. et al., 2014. Drawing on the right side of the brain: A voxel-based morphometry analysis of observational drawing. *Neuroimage,* August, Volume 96, pp. 167-173.

Charlesworth, J., 2011. *Maple Hayes Hall School,* Manchester: Office for Standards in Education, Children's Services and Skills.

Churchill, W. S., 1949. *The Second World War.* London: Cassell & Co. Ltd..

Coltheart, M., 2005. Modeling Reading: The Dual-Route Approach. In: M. J. Snowling & C. Hulme, eds. *The Science of Reading: A Handbook.* Oxford: Blackwell, pp. 6-23.

Coltheart, M. et al., 2001. DRC: A Dual Route Cascaded Model of Visual Word Recognition and Reading Aloud. *Psychological Review,* 108(1), pp. 204-256.

Davis Dyslexia Association International, 2012. *Using Visual Imagery for Reading Comprehension.* [Online]
Available at: http://www.dyslexia.com/?p=2339
[Accessed 28 August 2016].

Davis, R. D., 1985. *The Cause of Dyslexia: Anatomy of a Learning Disability.* [Online]
Available at: https://www.dyslexia.com/davis-difference/davis-theory/the-cause-of-dyslexia/
[Accessed 31st October 2016].

Davis, R. D. & Braun, E. M., 2003. *The Gift of Learning: Proven New Methods for Correcting ADD, Math & Handwriting Problems.* August 2003 ed. New York: Perigee / Penguin Putnam.

de Saussure, F., [1916] 1959. *Course in General Linguistics.* New York: The Philosophical Library.

Dyslexic Advantage, 2015. *Redefining Dyslexia Based On Strengths.* [Online]
Available at:
http://www.dyslexicadvantage.org/redefining-dyslexia-based-on-strengths/
[Accessed 30 May 2016].

Ellis, A., 1957. Rational Psychotherapy and Individual Psychology.. *Journal of Individual Psychology,* Volume 13, pp. 38-44.

Engelbrecht, R. J., 2005. *The effect of the Ron Davis programme on the reading ability and psychological functioning of children.* [Online]
Available at: http://bin.ddai.us/dys/docs/Engelbrecht-2005-Masters-Thesis.pdf
[Accessed 29 October 2016].

Faber, A. & Mazlish, E., 2012. *How to Talk So Kids Will Listen & Listen So Kids Will Talk.* February 2012 ed. New York: Simon and Schuster.

Fawcett, A. & Nicolson, R., 2004. Dyslexia: the role of the cerebellum. *Electronic Journal of Research in Educational Psychology,* 2(2), pp. 35-58.

Frith, U. & Frith, C., 1998. Modularity of Mind and Phonological Deficit. In: C. von Euler, I. Lundberg & R. R. Llinas, eds. *Basic Mechanisms in Cognition and Language.* Amsterdam: Elsevier, pp. 3-17.

Gabrieli, J. D. E., 2009. Dyslexia: A New Synergy Between Education and Cognitive Neuroscience. *Science,* 17 July, Volume 325, pp. 280 - 283.

Gavin, P., 2015. *Audio Excerpts from the speech given by Heinrich Himmler to SS Group Leaders in Posen, occupied Poland.* [Online]
Available at:
http://www.historyplace.com/worldwar2/holocaust/h-posen.htm
[Accessed 19 10 2015].

Geschwind, N. & Galaburda, A. M., 1987. *Cerebral Lateralization: biological mechanisms, associations and pathology..* 1987 ed. Cambridge(Massachusetts): MIT Press.

Godsland, S., n.d. *Dyslexia Demystified.* [Online]
Available at: http://www.dyslexics.org.uk/
[Accessed 21 October 2015].

Goleman, D., 1996. *Emotional Intelligence.* 1996 ed. London: Bloomsbury Publishing plc.

Google, n.d. *Google Books Ngram viewer.* [Online]
Available at: https://books.google.com/ngrams
[Accessed 1 July 2015].

Griffin, J. & Tyrrell, I., 2001. *The APET model: standing cognitive therapy on its head.* [Online]
Available at: http://www.hgi.org.uk/resources/delve-our-extensive-library/mental-health-services-nhs-cbt-psychotherapy/apet-model
[Accessed 30th October 2016].

Hallowell, E. M. & Ratey, J. J., 2005. *Delivered from Distraction.* First Edition ed. New York: Ballantine Books.

Hartmann, T., 2007. *Hunters and Farmers Five Years Later.* [Online]
Available at: http://www.thomhartmann.com/articles/2007/11/hunters-and-farmers-five-years-later
[Accessed 29 July 2016].

Hartmann, T., 2007. *Thom Hartmann's Hunter and Farmer Approach to ADD/ADHD.* [Online]
Available at:

http://www.thomhartmann.com/articles/2007/11/thom-hartmanns-hunter-and-farmer-approach-addadhd
[Accessed 31 July 2016].

International Dyslexia Association, 2015. *Effective Reading Instruction.* [Online]
Available at: https://dyslexiaida.org/effective-reading-instruction/
[Accessed 18th July 2017].

Jacobson, L. A. et al., 2011. Working Memory Influences Processing Speed and Reading Fluency in ADHD. *Child Neuropsychology,* 17(3), pp. 209-224.

Kelly, M., 2015. *[Senco-forum] phonics success?.* [Online]
Available at:
http://lists.education.gov.uk/pipermail/senco-forum/2015-July/017049.html
[Accessed 21 October 2015].

Kim, J. S., 2008. Research and the Reading Wars. In: *When research matters: How scholarship influences education policy..* Cambridge(Massachusetts): Harvard Education Press, pp. 89 - 111.

Kirby, J. R. & Bowers, P. N., 2012. *Morphology Works.* [Online]
Available at:
www.edu.gov.on.ca/eng/literacynumeracy/inspire/research/whatWorks.html
[Accessed 21 October 2015].

Koestler, A., 1964. *The Act of Creation.* London: Hutchinson & Co..

Kramer, S., 2016. Is there a link between perceptual talent and dyslexia?. *The Journal of Inclusive Practice in further and higher education,* Issue 7, pp. 34-48.

Lazar, S. W. et al., 2005. Meditation experience is associated with increased cortical thickness. *Neuroreport,* 28 November, 16(17), pp. 1893-1897.

LeDoux, J. E., 2002. Emotion, Memory and the Brain. *Scientific American,* April, 12(1), pp. 62-71.

Lyle, S., 2014. The limits of phonics teaching. *School Leadership Today,* 10 02, Volume 5.5, pp. 68 - 74.

Mackay, D. G. et al., 2004. Relations between emotion, memory, and attention: Evidence from taboo Stroop, lexical decision, and immediate memory tasks. *Memory & Cognition,* 32(3), pp. 474-488.

Marshall, A., 2003. *Brain Scans Show Dyslexics Read Better with Alternative Strategies.* [Online]
Available at: http://www.dyslexia.com/science/different_pathways.htm
[Accessed 09 July 2015].

National Literacy Trust, n.d. *The Secondary Quick Guide to Phonics.* [Online]
Available at: http://www.literacytrust.org.uk/assets/0002/3523/Sample_section_secondary_phonics_guide.pdf
[Accessed 08 July 2015].

Oxford University Press, n.d. *Oxford Dictionary of English,* Brighton: WordWeb Software.

Pfeiffer, S. et al., 2001. The Effect of the Davis Learning Strategies on First Grade Word Recognition and Subsequent Special Education Referrals. *Reading Improvement,* 38(2).

Pfeiffer, S. et al., 2001. The Effect Of The Davis Learning Strategies On First Grade Word Recognition And Subsequent Special Education Referrals. *Reading Improvement,* 38(2), pp. 74 - 84.

Pinker, S., 1999. *How The Mind Works.* Kindle edition ed. London: Penguin Books.

Pinker, S., 2008. *The Stuff of Thought: Language as a Window into Human Nature.* London: Penguin Books.

Rayfield, D., 2005. *Stalin and His Hangmen: An Authoritative Portrait of a Tyrant and Those Who Served Him.* London: Penguin.

Reynolds, C. R. & Bigler, E. D., 2007. *Test of Memory and Learning - Second Edition.* Austin(Texas): Pro-Ed Inc..

Rose, S. J., 2009. *Identifying and Teaching Children and Young People with Dyslexia and Literacy Difficulties,* London: Department for Children, Schools and Families.

Savage, R., Carless, S. & Erten, O., 2009. The longer-term effects of reading interventions delivered by experienced teaching assistants. *Support for Learning,* May, 24(2), pp. 95-100.

Schurz, M. et al., 2015. Resting-State and Task-Based Functional Brain Connectivity in Developmental Dyslexia. *Cerebral Cortex,* October, 25(10), pp. 3502-3514.

Shaywitz, S. E., Mody, M. & Shaywitz, B. A., 2006. Neural Mechanisms in Dyslexia. *Current Directions in Psychological Science,* 15(6), pp. 278-281.

Smith, A., 1982. *Symbol Digit Modalities Test.* Torrance(CA): Western Psychological Services.

Snowling, M. J., 2000. *Dyslexia.* 2000 ed. Oxford: Blackwell Publishers Ltd..

Stein, J., 2001. The magnocellular theory of developmental dyslexia. *Dyslexia,* Jan - Mar, 7(1), pp. 12-36.

Stroop, J. R., 1935. Studies of interference in serial verbal reactions.. *Journal of Experimental Psychology,* 18(6), pp. 643-662.

Sweitzer, L., 2014. *The Elephant in the ADHD Room: Beating Boredom as the Secret to Managing ADHD.* 2014 ed. London: Jessica Kingsley Publishers.

Tressoldi, P. E. et al., 2003. Confronto di efficacia ed efficienza tra trattamenti per il miglioramento della lettura in soggetti dislessic.. *Psicologia Clinica Dello Sviluppo,* VII(3), pp. 481-493.

Turner, M., 1994. Sponsored Reading Failure. In: *Language, Literacy and Learning in Educational Practice.* Clevedon: Multilingual Matters Ltd., pp. 111 - 127.

Tzivanakis, I., 2003. Links oder rechts? Auf der Suche nach einer Problemdefinition.. *The Dyslexic Reader,* 30(1), pp. 15-17.

UK Literacy Association, 2012. *Analysis of Schools' response to the Year 1 Phonics Screening Check,* Leicester: UK Literacy Association.

van Staden, A., Tolmie, A. & Badenhorst, M., 2009. Enhancing intermediate dyslexic learners' literacy skills: a Free State community project.. *Africa Education Review,* October, 6(2), pp. 295-307.

von Károlyi, C. & Winner, E., 2004. Dyslexia and Visual Spatial Talents: Are They Connected?. In: T. M. Newman & R. J. Sternberg, eds. *Students with Both Gifts and Learning Disabilities: Identification, Assessment, and Outcomes.* New York: Springer Science+Business Media, pp. 95-118.

Ward, H., 2010. *Is the zort-and-koob reading test for six-year-olds simply too monstrous?.* [Online]
Available at:
https://www.tes.co.uk/article.aspx?storycode=6064219
[Accessed 10 July 2015].

Whitehead, P., 2016. *How Homeschooling Set Me Free to Love My ADHD.* [Online]
Available at:
http://www.additudemag.com/adhdblogs/30/12019.html
[Accessed 30th October 2016].

Wilce, H., 2011. *One-to-one makes all the difference when teaching children to read.* [Online]
Available at:
http://www.independent.co.uk/news/education/schools/one-to-one-makes-all-the-difference-when-teaching-children-to-read-977889.html
[Accessed 22 October 2015].

Winter, C., 2015. *The Virtual 'Caliphate': Understanding Islamic State's Propaganda Strategy.* [Online] Available at: http://www.quilliamfoundation.org/ [Accessed 19 10 2015].

Zylowska, L., Ackerman, D. L., May, H. & Yang, J., 2008. Mindfulness Meditation Training in Adults and Adolescents With ADHD. *Journal of Attention Disorders,* May, 11(6), pp. 737-746.

INDEX

additional time allowance, 33, 81
Additude magazine, 81
amygdala, 100
Ariely, Dan, 101
Attention Deficit Hyperactivity Disorder, 80–94
Baddeley, Alan and Hitch, Graham, 108
behavioural economics, 101
British Dyslexia Association, 57
Churchill, Winston, 46
cognitive behavioural therapy, 100
conceptual wisdom, 45–47
connectives, 3, 45, 50, 75
Davis, Ronald, 7, 87, 89, 103
Davis Alphabet Mastery technique, 105, 111
Davis Concept Mastery, 152
Davis Learning Strategies, 71, 116–23
Davis Orientation Counseling, 87–88
Davis Symbol Mastery, 128–43
Davis Symbol Mastery procedure, 31, 128–43
de Saussure, Ferdinand, 37
Dial procedure, 125
disorientation, 87, 103–4
Dual Route Cascaded Model', 12
Dual-Route hypothesis of reading fluency, 12
dyslexia, hypotheses of, 97–98
Dyslexic Advantage, 6
Einstein, Albert, 42
experiential mastery, 200

Faber, Adele and Mazlish, Elaine, 91
Faraday, Michael, 42
Focus procedure, 124
Godsland, Susan, 53, 57
Goleman, Daniel, 100, 101
grapheme-phoneme correspondence, 8, 12, 44, 64
Hallowell, Edward, 89
Hartmann, Thom, 83–85
Human Givens Institute, 100
internal monologue, 13
Islamic State, 47
Joint Council for Qualifications, 81
Kekulé, August, 42
Kim, James, 52
Kindle reading device, 72
Knickebein technology (World War II), 46
Kramer, Sara, 6
LeDoux, Joseph, 100, 101
left/right awareness, 104–5
letter names, 65–67
letter reversals, 104
Lyle, Sue, 50
Major, John, 40
Mann, Horace, 52
Maple Hayes Dyslexia School, 56–57
Marshall, Abigail, 11–12
mathematics, 45
meridian, 163
metre standard, origin, 156
mindfulness, 86–87, 111
morphological approaches to reading, 54–56
multisensory learning techniques, 26, 67, 75, 111, 119, 180, 181, 192
Nietzsche, Friedrich, 37
North Yorkshire Reading Intervention, 10
orientation, 87
Pavlik Morozov legend (Maxim Gorky), 47
phonic reading instruction, 8–9, 45, 50, 51, 58
pictorial mind maps, 29–31
Picture-At-Punctuation, 146–50
Picture-At-Punctuation technique, 26
Pinker, Steven, 41, 42, 74
place value (mathematics), 180–91
punctuation awareness, 78
reading error analysis, 4
Reading Wars, 52, 53, 61

Release procedure, 124, 125–27
Rose, Sir Jim, 10, 38
Savage, Robert, 10
scaled scores, 111
Schurz, Matthias, 6
semiotics, 37
sight words, 76
Smith, Caroline, 19
speed of processing, 81
spelling, 105
Spell-Reading, 71, 144–46
Stroop Effect, 73–74
Symbol Digit Modalities Test, 82
synthetic phonics, 53
Test of Memory and Learning (Second Edition), 110
The Gift of Dyslexia (Davis, Ronald), 125, 146
The Gift of Learning (Davis, Ronald), 153
three parts of a word, 14, 58
Turner, Martin, 52
visualisation for learning, 31, 44
visual-sequential letter recognition, 65
Von Károlyi, Catya, 6
Whitehead, Philip, 92–94
whole word reading teaching, 52, 64
Winner, Ellen, 6
working memory, 108–11
Zylowska, Lydia, 86–87

Going Further

The Gift of Dyslexia by Ronald Davis

Written by a dyslexic who by his own efforts discovered how to overcome the barrier to reading, this book sets out the practical step-by-step techniques, using visualization and multisensory learning, which helped him to read and have since helped more than a thousand dyslexic children and adults. More than that - for the first time the experience of being dyslexic is fully explained, from its early development to its gradual entrenchment as a child comes to rely on non-verbal perception. Dyslexics will instantly identify with the author's descriptions of confusion and disorientation, and will recognize the 'trigger' words that make comprehension difficult.

These revelations should be read by all teachers, educational psychologists and parents.

https://www.dyslexia.com/book/the-gift-of-dyslexia/

Getting Help through the Davis® Methods

Davis Program Facilitators help people who struggle with:

- Reading
- Spelling
- Writing
- Math

- Time-Keeping
- Attention focus
- Organization
- Coordination

Davis Autism Providers help people with autism.

To Search For A Davis Provider Near You, Go To:

https://www.davismethod.org/

Licensed and certified by Davis Dyslexia Association International

Professional services described as Davis®, including Davis Dyslexia Correction®, Davis Symbol Mastery®, Davis Orientation Counseling®, Davis® Attention Mastery, Davis® Math Mastery, and Davis® Reading Program for Young Learners may only be provided by persons who are trained and licensed as Davis Facilitators or Specialists by Davis Dyslexia Association International.

Davis®, Davis Autism Approach®, Davis® Stepping Stones, and Davis® Concepts for Life are trademarks of Ronald D. Davis. Commercial use of these trademarks to identify educational, instructional, or therapeutic services requires licensing by the trademark owner.

Professional Training – for Teachers and Proactive Parents

WORKSHOP OUTLINE

How can a gift cause a problem?
Dyslexic giftedness
Multi-dimensional thinking

Preparing yourself to learn
Managing your mind:
'Pay attention!' 'But how?'

Why *Tyrannosaurus* But Not *If*?
Verbal vs. non-verbal thinking
Symbols vs. meaning in learning
The problem with *if*

Picture-At-Punctuation
Punctuation as a *reading* skill
Visualization for reading comprehension
Retention of what has been read

Davis Symbol Mastery

Creative exercise
Reading: filling in the blanks
Making subject vocabulary 'stick'

Three Stages of Learning

Assimilation – storage – retrieval
Managing the mind for assimilation
Some ideas for storage
The final touch: retrieval

Who should attend?

- ✓ SENCOs
- ✓ Learning Support teachers
- ✓ classroom teachers (primary and secondary)
- ✓ private tutors
- ✓ parents
- ✓ anyone interested in learning processes

For details of workshops near you, go to
https://www.davistraining.info/

The *Gift of Dyslexia* Workshop

The **Gift of Dyslexia Workshop** is a four-day introduction to the basic theories, principles and application of all the procedures described in Ronald Davis's internationally best-selling book, The Gift of Dyslexia, and more. Training is done with a combination of lectures, demonstrations, group practice, and question and answer sessions.

Participants will learn:

- How the Davis procedures were developed.

- How to screen for the 'gift of dyslexia' and establish a symptoms profile.

- How to help dyslexics eliminate perceptual disorientation and focus their attention.

- Special techniques for working with people who do not visualize well or have ADHD symptoms.

- How to incorporate and use proven methods for reducing confusion and mistakes in a classroom, home-schooling, tutoring or therapeutic setting.
- How to structure a Davis Dyslexia Program.

Who Should Attend?

- ✓ Parents
- ✓ Home educators
- ✓ Teachers
- ✓ Special Ed Coordinators
- ✓ Special Ed Support Staff
- ✓ Tutors
- ✓ Psychologists
- ✓ Counselors
- ✓ Speech therapists
- ✓ Occupational Therapists
- ✓ Trainers
- ✓ Researchers
- ✓ Career Guidance Counsellors
- ✓ Anyone interested in helping others correct their dyslexia

For details of workshops near you, go to
https://www.davistraining.info/

Would you like to ...

- Reach all the children in your class, regardless of their learning style?
- Manage your classroom more effectively?
- Have methods that are easy to implement and flexible?
- Meet early intervention reading needs that <u>prevent</u> the onset of SpLD?

DAVIS Learning Strategies

– the missing piece...

A Breakthrough in Primary Education
based on six years of classroom piloting and research.

"The creative process and the learning process, if not the same thing, are so closely associated, we will never be able to separate them."

- Ronald Davis

For further details, and to find out how to bring Davis Learning Strategies to your school, go to

https://www.davislearn.com

"I don't understand it:

He can read *'tyrannosaurus'*, but he gets stuck on *'if'*!!"

Would you like to:

- Grasp the reasons why some bright children may struggle to acquire basic academic skills;
- Use these insights to make an incisive difference to the abilities, well-being and prospects of these children in your classroom;
- Acquire insights and approaches that enable you to stimulate both academically able and academically challenged children at the same time;
- Give disruptive and impulsive children better control of their focus and behavior;
- Make a valuable difference to children who, while they may be academically able, have difficulty in areas such as sitting still, controlling hand-eye coordination, succeeding at sports, learning from consequences, or reading people?

Sign up to my *free* online course for teachers and parents and struggling learners. Ask your child's teachers to sign up too.

www.whytyrannosaurusbutnotif.com

Richard Whitehead

Richard originally discovered the Davis methods when looking for a solution for the son of some friends. He is a Davis Workshop Presenter and Training Specialist and has delivered lectures and teaching workshops on the Davis methods in countries as diverse as Iceland, Estonia, Ireland, Italy, Portugal, Poland, the United States, India, South Africa, New Zealand and Israel.

Richard's extensive background in education has included time spent teaching in both the adult and mainstream secondary educational sectors. He is currently Special Educational Needs Coordinator at a flourishing independent secondary boarding school in Worcestershire, UK and is a licensed Specialist SpLD Teacher Assessor. An Oxford-educated linguist with a working knowledge of several European languages, he specializes in multilingual learning disability assessments for non-native speakers of English in the UK.

Richard is author of a fifteen-part e-mentoring course for teachers of struggling learners which shares the same name as this book. He has written articles on the dyslexic learning style for publications as diverse as Literacy Today, Green Parent Magazine and Personnel Today magazine and has recorded video presentations on dyslexia for the *Dystalk* project.

www.ingramcontent.com/pod-product-compliance
Lightning Source LLC
Chambersburg PA
CBHW071229080526
44587CB00013BA/1544